Praise for *From Chaos to Connection*

"Whatever the present state of your marriage, it can always be better: more supportive, connected, loving, and caring. Reading *From Chaos to Connection* is like sitting down with a seasoned counselor who understands the dynamics of building a healthy marriage. The book stimulates the 'Yes, we can make things better' attitude. It is a hope-filled book for all who want a growing marriage."

—Gary D. Chapman, PhD, author of *The 5 Love Languages*

"Lori Epting has written an intriguingly fun book about marriage counseling. I didn't think you could write an entertaining guide to couples' healing, but Lori gets both the love and the pain of relationships. She understands that our culture expects us to spend more time on work and our kids' activities than on ourselves and our relationships. She gets that even the best marriages can be very difficult, [and] empathy and better communication can help any couple survive the madness. That is what this book is about."

—Robert Weiss, PhD, LCSW, CSAT, chief clinical officer
of Seeking Integrity Treatment Centers and author of
Prodependence: Moving Beyond Codependency,
among other books

"Blunt, brave, and bold! *From Chaos to Connection* is a must-read. I laughed, I cried, and I now look at my marriage and husband in a completely new light . . . despite being happily married for eighteen years! I highly recommend this entertaining and enlightening read to all overwhelmed and overworked couples looking to save their sanity and their marriages."

—Katherine Wintsch, founder & CEO of The Mom
Complex and author of *Slay Like a Mother*

More praise for *From Chaos to Connection*

"*From Chaos to Connection* is a straightforward, down-to-earth book willing to challenge your ideas of marriage. Lori's personal writing style, as she courageously weaves her own personal and marital story into her writing, makes for an engaging read. She invites couples to reconsider common relationship dilemmas as opportunities for a deeper, more compassionate view of their relationship."

—Marcus R. Earle, PhD, LMFT, CSAT, S-PSB, clinical director of Psychological Counseling Services, Ltd.

"This book is a wonderful resource, one that I wish I had at my disposal before my first marriage ended. The author entwines details from her personal life with her training as a marriage therapist, making her advice both helpful and relatable. I think her "What's the Real Problem—A Cheat Sheet" was invaluable, and can be applied to any marriage. This is a must-read for parents trying to navigate the stressors of both marriage and parenthood. Highly recommended!"

—Tara Egan, DEd, child therapist and author of *Adolescence: A Parent's Guide*

"*From Chaos to Connection* will take you on a rare journey into both the heart and mind of a thoughtful and skilled couples therapist. With both vulnerability and humor, Lori Epting not only takes us into her therapy practice, but into her own marriage. The lessons [it provides] about love and relationships are relevant, well-founded, and brilliantly woven throughout the book."

— Marni Feuerman, MSW, PsyD, psychotherapist and author of *Ghosted and Breadcrumbed: Stop Falling for Unavailable Men and Get Smart about Healthy Relationships*

FROM *Chaos* TO CONNECTION

A MARRIAGE COUNSELOR'S CANDID GUIDE FOR THE MODERN COUPLE

LORI EPTING, L.C.M.H.C

BELLE ISLE BOOKS
www.belleislebooks.com

ISBN: 978-1-951565-93-0
LCCN: 2020909598

Cover and interior designed by Michael Hardison
Project managed by Erin Harpst

Author photo (p. 249) by Bryan Bazemore

Printed in the United States of America

Published by
Belle Isle Books (an imprint of Brandylane Publishers, Inc.)
5 S. 1st Street
Richmond, Virginia 23219

BELLE ISLE BOOKS
www.belleislebooks.com

belleislebooks.com | brandylanepublishers.com

Dedicated to the struggling couples who are
bravely and courageously finding time
—when there seems to be none—
to fight for their marriages.

Table of Contents

Preface

As a couples therapist, I have the privilege of walking with couples through their hardships. It truly is an honor. Couples allow me into their most sacred spaces, spaces they themselves have a hard time going through with each other. They let me examine their feelings, experiences, and issues that they may not have shared with anyone else in their lives. They put their faith in me, trusting that I can help, and I am grateful for it.

Throughout my years as a therapist, I have seen the same problems show up over and over in distressed couples. Again and again, I hear couples using the same words to describe their problems. Couples often come to therapy feeling unique—different—broken. And then I tell them that their problems are so normal. They are the struggles that thousands of other couples also face each day. And most importantly, they are often fixable.

Your relationship distress is not unique—in fact, it's normal, familiar, even expected. And it can be fixed.

This book is the culmination of all my experience, research, and training. In it, I lay out the familiar problems and patterns that create distress, loneliness, heartache, and distance between couples. I give these problems and patterns names: Bill and Amy,

Deborah and Mike, or Cindy and Anthony. These aren't the real names of the couples who have come to me with these problems—just the names I put on particular problems that have presented themselves hundreds of times in my office.

The words in this book are a synthesis of all my clients and experience. Whether you are one of my clients, a friend, or someone I have never met, it is my hope that when you read these words, they feel familiar. Perhaps they might even be words you yourself have said or thought at times.

I hope you find yourself in these pages. I hope that the stories resonate—and most of all, I hope that this book provides you with the hope, the reassurance, and the tools you need to help your relationship thrive.

Introduction

As a marriage counselor, I can sit in a room with a screaming couple and not break a sweat. I can listen with ease to arguments over who has been more wronged, who isn't being appreciated, and who didn't remember to let the dog out last night. I eagerly sit on the edge of my seat without so much as a heart palpitation as a spouse rants about the failings of their partner. However, if you want to spike my blood pressure and put me into a cold sweat, ask me to be the room-mom for my two-year-old's preschool class and arrange a Pinterest-worthy Valentine's Day party, complete with cutesy cards for her classmates who can't even read yet. You could watch the shame creep over me as I scour blogs and pins for respectable ideas while ignoring my husband's third request to "come to bed already."

I'll be the first to say it: modern marriage is for the birds. Take me back to the days of my parents, when there was no internet and no expectation of themed birthday parties complete with hashtags. Take me back to the days before there was a photographer's package for every holiday, and beautifully touched-up pictures that get posted on every single social media site and make the rest of us feel subpar about our marriages and families. Take me back to the days when married couples could be at the top of their parenting game just by checking their kids' report cards at the year's end and attending a PTA meeting every now and then. Take me back to the days when a person could just grab a few McDonald's Happy Meals without feeling like they were poisoning their family. Are we seriously supposed to stay happily married with our union securely intact through all this insanity? Modern marriage is crazy.

Let me start by sharing one of my "crazy" moments, the kind that could make or break any marriage. It was a Saturday morning. Saturday mornings are a perfect time for me to work as a marriage counselor, because my husband, Chad, is home to wrangle the kids. I can get myself ready distraction-free, and out the door in a peaceful manner—every mom's dream.

Now, this particular Saturday, I had arranged for our daughter's favorite babysitter to come over for about an hour so that my husband could play in a friendly neighborhood tennis match. At 6:30 a.m., the alarm clock went off, and he was out the door. I took a quick shower before my two-year-old and five-year-old woke up. Once they were up, I turned on *Doc McStuffins* so I could blow-dry my hair and get dressed. I put out some breakfast and a change of clothes for the kids. The clock was ticking, but . . . no babysitter.

Hmmm, I thought. *Maybe I told her to come at 8:30 instead of 8:15?* I checked my text messages. Nope, I'd actually told her 8:00.

It was 8:35. In exactly twenty-five minutes, my clients would be sitting in the waiting room at my office, and there was still no sign of the babysitter. I called and texted her. I called and texted my husband. No response from anyone. I started to panic.

This led to a series of events that ended with my neighbor answering the third of my frantic calls in the middle of her kick-boxing class. She proceeded to call her husband and uproot him from his couch, where he was spending a rare kid-free moment with his coffee, to get him to hustle up to my house. When he was within eyeshot, I jumped in my car, headed down the street to my babysitter's house, and banged on her door. (Yes, I have no shame.) She jumped out of bed and threw on her clothes, and we raced back to my house, where I dropped her at the end of the driveway.

As I sped down the road to work, Chad finally called me back. I heard him so innocently say, "Hey babe, I'm in between sets—did you need something?"

I wish I could tell you I used all my education, training, and experience as a marriage counselor to perfectly regain my composure and say, "I'm all good! It was a bit crazy, but I got it all worked out! Enjoy the rest of your match!" But no, the real ending to this story is that I laid into my husband with such theatrics that I may now be up for a Golden Globe Award. Seconds after getting off the phone, he emailed me the confirmation number for a two-hour massage he had scheduled for me for later that day. I'm not sure if that was his way of saying, "Sorry you had such a tough morning," or "I'm willing to pay hundreds of dollars for you to relax at a spa in the hopes you don't come home still acting like a crazy person."

Married life with kids is chaos. Even though I have counseled couples through a wide array of seemingly insurmountable marital trials and tribulations, I have to be honest: I can't completely eliminate the chaos that arises during this time of life. None of us— not even therapists—can avoid moments when the children are screaming, the dogs are barking, your phone is ringing, and your spouse is yelling for you, all while dinner is burning. So I can't help you get the lunches packed, get yourself looking halfway presentable, get out the door, take the kids to school, get to work on time, perform to your boss's standards, and leave work in time to get home without your spouse being upset that you missed dinner together. I can't help you keep the house clean, get the laundry done, put away the dishes, cook healthy meals, *and* squeeze in a workout, all while keeping the kids entertained and stimulated in a way that will help them grow into wonderful, thriving adults.

And I can't tell you exactly how to find sufficient time for yourself or your spouse amid all this chaos, either. You can plan more date nights, get more sitters, or call for reinforcement from the grandparents more often—but you already know that. Even with those "solutions," there is really no way to get around the craziness that becomes your life when it expands beyond just you.

There's a reason my office is filled with couples who are trying to raise thriving children and be unrealistically available to their families while balancing one or even two careers: it's really, really hard. And in American culture, parents typically are not given adequate support. It's not uncommon to live far from extended family and the support they offer, to have spouses who travel for work, and to be bombarded by social media and faced with expectations that make us want to crawl into a fetal position in bed. We scroll through Instagram feeds full of photos of perfectly dressed families laughing together over their homemade, organic, free-range-egg cupcake creations with the quote "Families who bake together stay together!" superimposed in fancy lettering over the pictures. If you ask Alexa how to balance career and family, she will direct you to eighteen pages of Google articles claiming to share the secret to achieving said balance. I would love it if Alexa would just shoot me straight and say, "Sorry, lady, balance is a myth. But can I interest you in contact information for a couple of good therapists, a spa, and some exceptional babysitting services?"

We are drowning under the pressures of modern parenting, and unfortunately, deteriorating marriages are often just part of the collateral damage. Instead of blaming our fast-paced culture full of ridiculous expectations, we can mistakenly blame our partners. We say, "You work too much—it's like I'm a single parent!" or "You are home all day—you have so much time to get things done! What do you have to complain about?" or "I'm exhausted when I get home from work—I just need a few minutes of downtime!" or "I'm exhausted from dealing with the kids all day—I just need some downtime!"

I wish we would look at the pressures around us and say to our partners, "Gosh, of course you're tired—you're overworked and underappreciated. Look at how hard you work for our family! Look at everything you're trying to manage! Of course you feel overwhelmed and exhausted! We're in this together."

I want to be clear, as your marriage counselor *pro tem:* modern parents should feel overwhelmed, exhausted, and like they are failing most of the time. Whether you are a stay-at-home parent, a parent who works full-time, or somewhere in between, what you are doing is ridiculously hard. And because it is hard, you need your spouse more than ever. Therefore, my goal is to help you achieve connection in your marriage—to help both of you feel that you are on the same team; that you have a life partner who has your back; that you are with someone you love, trust, find comfort in, and even want to have sex with—and *that,* I know how to do. I know the attitudes, strategies, and behaviors that can help keep your marriage intact during this whirlwind time of life.

I also know that couples can survive the most ridiculously insane moments and heartbreaking life stressors when they learn how to find each other beneath the big pile of busyness, poopy diapers, and vacations spent in urgent care. None of this requires the ability to respond in perfect ways to your perfectly attuned spouse. It just requires the ability to connect. Breathe a sigh of relief! You can be imperfect in your imperfect marriage and still find love, connection, and contentment. As we say in the South, God bless.

I wrote this book to give overwhelmed and overworked married people everywhere real, honest, and candid advice on how to find happiness in their marriage. Because let's be real: our culture sets us up to care more about losing our baby weight and schlepping our kids from activity to activity than about how we love our spouses. I wrote this book so you can learn how to experience the game-changing, unparalleled power of connecting with your spouse when life is racing by or running you over. With this skill intact, so is your marriage.

☙

When I first became a marriage counselor, I loved talking to people about my job. I love what I do. I love the feeling of turning a marriage around—of taking a couple full of pain, hurt, and loneliness, and watching them transform. I love hearing the words, "It's a miracle! I can't believe it's this good! Thank you."

However, there are times I don't want people to know what I do for a living. I know exactly how a physician must feel as she is checking out at the grocery store on the way home from work, still wearing her scrubs, and a stranger asks, "Can you take a look at this weird rash on my arm?" "Yuck!" she wants to respond. "No! I'm just trying to pick up milk and bread! Can I just do that without looking at your weird rash?"

The worst is airplanes. I always lie to people on airplanes about what I do. I've learned the hard way, after letting the super-chatty passenger sharing a row with me know my profession and being trapped beside her with no way out for the remainder of our four-hour flight. No way out of the stories of her friend's husband's cousin, who found out his wife was cheating on him, and that his son wasn't even his, "and can you believe she had the nerve to show up at the family reunion?" *Ummm . . . I can't. But can I go back now to my Kindle and my earphones and the book I just downloaded, because this is the only free time I'll have in the next year to actually be able to read a book without two kids crawling all over me?! Can I, please?!*

So I find it's much safer to say that I'm an accountant. People don't usually have a lot of interest in accounting. But they love to know about marriage counseling. I hear, "Oh, I bet you have some crazy stories!" Or, "I don't know how you do what you do. What's it like to hear all that misery?"

My clients are equally interested. They want to know about me. They say, "I bet you and your husband *never* have these kinds of problems!" Or, "I bet you go home and laugh over the dinner table about our silly fights." My favorite is when clients try to compare their level of dysfunction to my other clients'. They wonder whether I think, *Oh, no, not them!* when I see their names pop up on my schedule. They say, "I bet we sound ridiculous. I'm sure you have clients with *real* problems, and here we are, arguing over who left the dirty dishes in the sink."

So here it is: a tell-all. I'll take you inside my mind as a marriage counselor, inside my office with my clients, and behind the closed doors of my home. Because even though I can't escape the chaos of modern life, I may have a few things figured out about how to do this relationship thing after all. Because as we all know, marriage is hard.

But mine isn't.

I'm not bragging. I'm not patting myself on the back. I'm just being honest. My marriage is not hard. It's not exhausting. I'm not tired of repeating myself over and over while my husband doesn't change. I'm not tired of having the same fight over again. I'm not disillusioned and hopeless because I feel we are disconnected or may never be able to get to a good place again. I haven't lost trust in him. I haven't lost my attraction to him. I haven't started to wonder whether I made a terrible mistake marrying him, or started to think we have no hope because we are "just totally different people." I don't gaze at other men and strike up flirtatious conversations just to see if someone else would be interested in me. Our conversations do not center only on our children or on planning activities and meals. I haven't started to stay late at work because I dread coming home. I don't have to—because I have a happy marriage.

It's not that my husband and I haven't struggled at times. Actually, our biggest struggles occurred when we were dating. I still remember the day I met him—this cute, confident Midwestern boy—at a trendy sushi spot in Scottsdale, Arizona. He had a good job and good values, and came from a good family. I decided pretty quickly that he was the one for me. He, however, wanted to take things slowly. Due to this contrast, we were the couple who broke up and got back together twice—maybe even three times. He liked his independence, while I wanted more of a partnership. I wanted him to confess his undying love to me after three months (Seems reasonable, right?!), and he didn't want to rush things. The more I pushed, the more he pulled back, and the more he pulled back, the louder, more hostile and dramatic I got. It's actually quite the miracle that we made it to an engagement. But once we were on the road to marriage, things changed. We settled in, and things got . . . easy.

It's not that I think marriage should be easy. On the contrary, I think it is inherently difficult. It should require work. It should feel exhausting, frustrating, and unfulfilling at times. It should have ebbs and flows, good days and bad, days you want to kill each other and days you can't imagine life without each other. It should be hard, and if yours is, you are in good company. But it shouldn't feel hopeless and distant. If it does, then I am hopeful that the strategies in this book can turn it around.

Aside from my personal life, my professional journey paved the path to this book. I started my career working with divorced couples. I watched them fight endlessly over who got the kids on Fridays and who got to spend Christmas with the kids and who paid whom what. I saw people spend tens of thousands of dollars disputing their former spouse in court and lose years of their lives fighting about whether or not their young daughter should play soccer, or get a haircut. My experience made me settle on one truth: there has got to be a better way.

I can remember every time a couple have sat before me and told me that one of them has made the decision to leave the marriage. When this happens, I swear a piece of me dies. My heart aches for the incredible loss, and my body feels the pain of the spouse being left behind.

Years ago, one of my favorite clients was struggling with the overwhelming decision of whether to leave her loveless marriage or not. I watched as she painfully vacillated for months and months over what to do. One day (when I was seven months pregnant, mind you), she came into session and said she had made a decision. She was ending the marriage. Well, my pregnancy hormones apparently could not handle this revelation, and I burst out in tears. After apologizing profusely for my hormonal hysterics, I gently supported her decision. I also put off any other heartbreaking sessions until after my daughter was born.

Don't get me wrong—I know some relationships should end. Sometimes a relationship is so toxic that in order to protect one's personal safety and sanity, it is best to get out. But I also believe it is shortsighted and tragic to think that divorce will end one's problems. Often, it just replaces an old set of problems with new ones. I also believe that a failed marriage can leave a scar that takes an incredibly long time to heal.

This is my bias, because I have not been divorced, and I do not have divorced parents. I know plenty of people who have left bad marriages and later found a suitable partner or felt that they were in a better situation. Nonetheless, I believe that the bad habits of ended marriages often lead to bad habits in new ones. This is why, statistically, a second marriage can easily turn into a third or fourth.

However, I would not look at a couple celebrating their thirty-fifth wedding anniversary and automatically congratulate them for their "success." There is absolutely something to be said for sticking to one's commitment—but so many times, I have sat with a couple contemplating their next steps after thirty-five years of a miserable, loveless, empty marriage. In fact, most often, these couples have emotionally left each other a long time ago. They just didn't do it formally in the eyes of the law.

The truth is that both divorce and remaining in a hostile and loveless marriage leave their scars and create their own suffering. But when I sit with these couples and hear their stories of pain and misery, I think, *There has to be a better way.*

This is one of the reasons I have become eager to learn what helps a marriage succeed—so that I can help others. For me, there is no bigger joy in life than watching two people who have been mired in the depths of hopelessness and despair in their marriage turn it around. I really feel like I watch miracles happen in those moments when couples are willing to dive into their acute pain to save themselves from years of future suffering. I feel like a surgeon who has removed an inoperable tumor and has the opportunity to share the good news with the patient. I can't help it—I tear up every time.

I have written this book as someone who is fascinated with marriage and relationships, who has studied marriage both formally and informally, who has sat with couples who have been married for forty years or two years—or who have never married, or are engaged, or who have separated for the fifth time, or divorced for the second time. I've also (to my husband's chagrin) overanalyzed my own marriage, especially through the births of my two daughters, countless sleepless nights, and endless diapers. In doing so, I have learned that some of my strategies for maintaining a happy, fulfilling marriage are somewhat peculiar, even unexpected. Some may even defy conventional wisdom. However, my years of scrutiny have helped me and others create and maintain awesome marriages.

I've already done the obsessing. Let me tell you what I've learned.

How to Use This Book

In this book, I discuss the major factors that contribute to a successful marriage, as well as common pitfalls to achieving marital success. Each chapter tackles these factors separately. It is not necessary to read the chapters in order, and you may find it helpful to focus on the chapters that most closely pertain to you.

Finally, try not to fall into the trap of reading this book and noting whether your spouse does or doesn't do the things I describe. Instead, ask yourself whether you do or don't do those things. The most helpful way to read this book is through the lens of how *you* act in your marriage. Let me put it this way: you can strategically highlight one or two pages to leave in the bathroom for your spouse to read, but that's it. For the rest of the book, focus on yourself.

You Don't Need Good Communication

(Gasp!)

Yes, I said it: you don't need good communication to have a good marriage.

By this point, marriage experts from around the world are rolling over in their graves or have tossed this book onto the fire for warmth. But wait! Hear me out. I'm not saying you don't need to communicate. In fact, I've spent the better part of my time with couples being completely shocked at how little they talk to each other about anything. Simple questions such as "How are you?" and "How was your day?" stop making it into their daily or weekly dialogue. So yes, you do need to talk to each other. What I'm saying is that your words don't have to be communicated in poetically perfect ways.

Why Aren't My Nifty Communication Tools Working?

When I first started counseling couples, I spent a lot of time helping them communicate. I learned numerous techniques with cute little acronyms that I would teach to my couples over and over to help them improve their communication.

I was motivated to do so because *every* couple comes to marriage counseling stating that they need "better communication."

However, I noticed these catchy, witty communication techniques usually didn't stick. A couple might use them while they were in my office or for a few days after our session, but most often, they reverted to their old patterns within days.

I started to look into this a bit more, and observed how my husband and I talk to each other. Here is what I learned: we are extremely sarcastic. We take jabs at each other; we yell at times and shut down at other times. We nitpick and push each other's buttons. We misunderstand each other and react sensitively to perceived slights. We get upset if we feel unheard or ignored. We have the same fights over and over:

> *Chad: You said you were going to be home at seven.*
>
> *Me: I'm sorry; I got caught up in something at work.*
>
> *Chad: You didn't think to call?*
>
> *Me: Sorry, I was busy doing a bunch of stuff and trying to get out the door.*
>
> *Chad: It only takes five seconds to send a quick text— you don't have five seconds?*
>
> *Me: I'm sorry! I'll do it next time!*

Here's my confession: I won't remember to call the next time. Really, I won't. As a result, we've had this conversation close to three hundred times, and we will have this conversation when we are old and gray, because it doesn't change a thing: I'm always leaving the office later than I say, and because I'm late, I'm always scrambling to get out the door, and don't want to take the five seconds to text. End of story.

Here's another thing we do: we go to bed angry sometimes. In fact, I went to bed angry the night before I wrote this chapter. I know—this is supposed to be a major no-no! But guess what? The world didn't end, and neither did my marriage. It took me a while even to remember the content of our argument the next day.

It's okay to go to bed angry sometimes. You can't expect to resolve all your issues before the day's end. Sometimes you just need to get some sleep and try again tomorrow. There's no shame in that. In fact, it takes a wise person to say, "This is going nowhere fast. Let's sleep on it and talk about it tomorrow, when we're rested." Too many factors can cause an emotional conversation to go awry; it's not wise to let sleep deprivation be one of those factors.

As I coached my couples and observed my own patterns of communication with my husband, I started to feel somewhat like a hypocrite: I was teaching my clients to do something I didn't even do! I'm reactive, I'm sensitive, and I exaggerate. I get distracted and start texting or checking emails during a conversation. I don't feel like talking at times, and I give short answers. I interrupt him and tell him why his opinion is wrong. I shut down when I get frustrated and tell him "nothing" is wrong when he asks over and over. My husband can do all these things, too. But despite all these failings, my husband and I operated, and continue to operate, in a happy, secure, and fulfilling marriage.

I realized that either I was completely delusional, or I was missing something. I started to open up to the idea that communication doesn't have to be pretty, full of "'I' statements" and phrases like "Let me repeat this back to see if I got it right." Instead of working to perfect communication between partners, I started focusing on helping couples understand the emotions behind their disagreements.

And when I did this, an amazing thing happened. I started to see couples struggle and stutter, ramble, interrupt each other—and *still* manage to get to a place of connection. Notice I didn't say *agreement*—I said *connection*. It is far more powerful for two people to sit together and muddle through the emotions they feel during conflict than it is for them to agree all the time. In fact, couples *shouldn't* always agree. No two people are that similar.

As I implemented this new strategy, I watched highly successful, articulate, poised partners have ugly conversations about deeply important issues in their marriage and come to a place of connection (which I will talk a lot about how to do throughout this book). When they reached that point, an amazing thing happened: couples started to brainstorm creative solutions. These solutions were usually far better than any solution I could have provided, because they came from the couple. Their solutions fit them. They weren't being told what to do, and their solutions weren't cookie-cutter answers recommended to every couple who walked into my office. (After all, one solution *shouldn't* fit every couple.)

Sometimes, couples do need carefully designed strategies and clever acronyms to help them improve their conversational skills. Without them, they can get stuck in their own poor patterns of communication—and of course anything is better than doing the same thing over and over and expecting different results. I'm not saying these tools do not help, as they most certainly do—when they are used. But they must be used.

I used to teach couples how to communicate by using helpful little mats. They were supposed to step on different parts of the mats to help guide themselves through the communication process. In practice, however, my couples were more likely to throw the mats at each other during moments of intense domestic conflict than to use them in a productive manner. We'd spend all that time learning and practicing with them in our sessions, and then *bam!*—nothing. When they came into the next session, the conversation would go like this:

> *Couple: We had some horrible fights this week.*
>
> *Me: Did you try using your communication mats?*
>
> *Couple: We thought about it once—well, we thought about it as we were sitting in the waiting room here, thinking it probably would have helped.*
>
> *Me: Okay, then what kept you from using the mats in those moments?*
>
> *Couple: We don't know; we didn't think about it.*
>
> *Me (mentally banging head on wall): Let's try again.*

There is a reason they didn't think to use their new tool. The problem is, when emotions ignite and pain is raw and intense, the brain has a really hard time accessing these very logical techniques. Our brains get hijacked when we are in conflict with the nearest and dearest person in our lives.

When I see my couples in serious conflict, and each member of the couple feels that the conflict could threaten their relationship with the most important person in their life, they are in a state of life-and-death panic. In these moments of panic and fear of losing or disconnecting from your spouse, asking yourself to stop and rack your brain for the five-step communication process you learned during your last therapy session or from the last book you read is like asking someone who is running from a burning building to sit down and re-create the exit plan they saw in the hallway. When it feels like your life depends on it, you just act.

I've also seen couples who had wonderfully articulate, calm conversations, only to separate soon after. Sometimes, these calm conversations were an indication that emotions—both positive and negative—had already left the relationship. Therefore, both partners exhibited little reactivity in their communication, and an amazing ability to pull together coherent and cohesive thoughts—but they didn't have an amazing connection.

Forget Everything Else and Just Pick One Tool

I'm not saying communication doesn't matter, because it does. It matters tremendously. (I'll talk in later chapters about some marriage-killers that involve communication.) I'm just saying you can really botch it up at times.

My husband and I have a rule in our marriage: you always get a do-over. Always. That means that whenever you ask for a do-over, whatever was previously said should be considered null and void.

Now, you can't pull out the do-over every five seconds. It has to be used sparingly, so that it's genuine and believable. And often, the correction is still hard to believe. I often find myself wanting to hold my husband's feet to the fire over whatever he originally said when he was reactive. *That must be what he* really *meant!* No, it wasn't. It's what he said when his brain was hijacked. It's what he said after a long day's work, when he was tired and stressed and hungry. When he actually had five minutes to think about it or hear me out, he truly changed his mind. And in those moments, he reminds me, "You *have* to let me change my mind. It's the rule."

We once had this argument after taking our hyperactive two-year-old daughter Reagan to a friend's house for a cookout:

Me: Did you have a good time at the cookout?

Chad: It was fine. I didn't get to talk to anyone because I was chasing Reagan around the whole time. You probably had a better time than me.

Me: Really? The whole time. I didn't do anything? I just got to sit back, relax and chat with friends. Is that really how you see it?

Chad: Pretty much, yep.

Me: So I didn't feed her, push her on the swing, get her milk, play with her. Do you think I got to talk to anyone either? But yes, you are right, you did everything, and I did nothing.

Chad: Okay, maybe I didn't notice what you were doing. I'm sure you were helping.

Me: Apparently not enough.

Chad: Look, I take it back. I get a do-over.

Me (I always seem to have one rebuttal to a do-over): No, no, no, you are right. I was totally unhelpful.

Chad: I said I'm calling a do-over. I was wrong. You were helpful. She's just a tough kid.

Me: Okay. I accept your do-over.

Now, don't go throwing away all the self-help books on communication that you bought to help you get through the petty, day-to-day arguments. Actually, do the opposite. Look over your bookshelf and pick out that one that you like best, and pick one thing out of it to remember—one thing that you may have a chance of remembering when you are in the throes of an emotional fight. For us, it's the do-over. Pick yours.

When It Comes to Communication, Imperfection Is Okay. Annihilation Is Not.

I could give countless examples of how communication can be unbelievably imperfect, but still turn out okay. My husband gave me a great example one weekend when he made work plans after he had already committed to keeping the kids. This gets me every time. I transform from my wise, poised marriage therapist self into a drama queen in seconds:

> *Chad: Hey, I agreed to work late tomorrow night. Okay?*
>
> *Me: What? I already made plans, remember? You are supposed to come home to be with the kids. Is it not on your calendar? You always seem to remember plans when they are for you, but when it comes to something I need, you forget to even put it on your calendar. I guess I'll cancel my plans, because they are obviously not important to you. Thanks a lot.*

Now, at this moment, my husband could say, "Chill out, Crazy Train. This isn't a big deal." But instead, he says something else:

Chad: You're right, I did promise. I'll cancel my client meeting.

Me: No. I'd hate for you to have to do that. I'll just call a sitter. I don't mind.

Chad: I really have no problem rescheduling. I'm sure it won't be a problem.

Me: No, really, it's okay. The kids will enjoy the sitter anyway.

Even though I presented myself as a whiny fourteen-year-old whose parents had told her she couldn't go out with her friends that night, he still listened. He still considered the information. He stayed open to my needs. And as he was open to my needs, I became sensitive to his needs and felt a desire to meet them.

Now, notice that I didn't hit him over the head with a pan or say, "You're a selfish piece of crap!" and "This is why you're a terrible husband." I didn't launch into a full-frontal assault, attacking his manhood or his sense of self-worth. You don't have to be a communication expert to work through conflict, but you *do* have to refrain from annihilating the other person. Examples of annihilation include (but are not limited to) name-calling, ranting, raging, attacking someone's character (e.g. "You are so selfish!"), storming out, and slamming doors.

If you find you cannot get through conflict without resorting to these tactics, go see a therapist. Seriously. Stop trying to muscle through—this is bigger than both of you. Let someone help you. If you are regularly making each other feel like big piles of crap, you need some intervention. There is a better way. It doesn't need to feel like this.

We All Sound Crazy at Times

I think it is important to know that we *all* get on the crazy train at times. The difference between happy and unhappy couples is that happy couples find it easier to get *off* that train. During moments of discord, she may feel, *He is so selfish. He only cares about himself. It's all about him. He couldn't care less about what I feel or what I need. He only thinks about Number One.* He may think, *She is so unappreciative. She doesn't realize all I do for us. She is never happy with me; it doesn't matter what I do.* But after couples learn how to respond to these normal feelings and thoughts effectively, they begin to feel differently. Even as they feel slighted and upset, they know in their hearts that their spouse does care.

For me, these crazy-train thoughts surface every time my family prepares to go on a trip. My husband brings down his small, neatly packed suitcase and says, "I'm ready; are you guys all ready?" I want to scream at him (and often do): "No! We are *not* ready! Did you think to pack the swim diapers, or the loveys, or the girls' toothbrushes? How about the beach towels and sunscreen, or the infant ibuprofen, or the puddle jumpers? Actually, did you think about *anything* apart from your golf clubs, tennis racquet, and bocce ball set? I have to pack for three people, but you only look out for Number One! Must be nice!"

But here is the reality: he *has* thought about us. He has already cleaned out the car, filled it up with gas, adjusted the car seats, taken the running stroller to the gas station to put air in the tires, and packed the beach chairs and umbrella. But in that moment, when both kids are hanging onto my legs and yelling "Mommy!" in harmony while I'm trying to find the matching tops to fit their sippy cups (the bane of my existence), I feel that everything falls to me. And I'm quick to let him know that.

Now, this could turn into a blowout fight within seconds. In fact, here's a conversation I often hear between couples who come in for counseling:

> *Husband (throwing car keys and going to sit on the couch and watch TV): Fine, do it yourself, then!*
>
> *Wife: I will! I already do anyway, so what's the difference?!*
>
> *Husband (to himself):* She is always nagging. She doesn't appreciate anything I do. In fact, it doesn't matter what I do, because nothing is ever enough for her. I basically suck as a husband, so why even bother? I may as well sit here and catch up on ESPN's *SportsCenter,* because even if I try, I get yelled at.
>
> *Wife (to herself):* There he is, watching *SportsCenter* again. He gets to do whatever he wants, while I do *everything* around here. He obviously doesn't care about me or our family. I don't know why I put up with this!

Now, here is how this situation plays out in my marriage:

> *Chad (spitefully and sarcastically): Actually, I already cleaned out the car, got gas, adjusted the car seats, filled up the tires of the jogging stroller, and packed the beach stuff. But yes, you are right, I only think about myself!*
>
> *Me: You did? Well, that's awesome. Thank you.*

*Seriously, thank you. I didn't realize you did all that.
I'm sorry. Do you accept my apology?*

Chad (still spiteful and short): It's fine. No big deal.

*Me: No, seriously, I am sorry. Thank you. (I give him a
kiss on his cheek.) Will you forgive me?*

Chad (a little more softly): Yes, I do.

(And he kisses me back.)

Me: I really am sorry.

Now, notice something here. This was a stupid, petty little fight that made no difference in the world, and I still had to apologize three times in this one conversation to make an impact, to soften my husband and convince him I was genuinely sorry. Three times! One of the things that strikes me is that my couples will go through huge blowouts or major betrayals, disappointments, or breaks in trust, and may never say, "I'm sorry." More likely, I hear, "I said I'm sorry. I don't know what else you expect me to do! You just need to get over it." Or, "I said I'm sorry, but she just keeps bringing it up over and over and over again. Enough already! She just needs to move on and quit dwelling on it!"

Now, in this shortsighted husband's defense, he is right—to an extent. She does need to move on. I promise, she desperately wants to, despite what he thinks. Often, I hear, "I think she wants to stay stuck on it; I think she likes to be miserable and make me miserable." I can promise you, she doesn't. She just doesn't know how to move on, how to keep your hurtful words, actions, and insults from feeling like a punch in the stomach or a dagger in her heart. She does not want to feel this way.

So here is a hard truth: you may need to apologize over and over again, especially if you've committed a true betrayal of trust. Did you get emotionally involved with a coworker? Did your spouse catch you in a lie? Did you hurl a verbal insult to your partner's character in a heated moment? If you did, you will need to apologize many times over, from a place of true sadness and contrition. She has to feel that you are sorry. She has to see it on your face—see a tear in your eye, a look of sadness, something that will let her realize how pained you are to have caused pain in her. And she may need to see this many times before it finally sinks in.

When a person gets hurt, they put up a wall. For some, this wall is light and spongy, and can be torn down easily, allowing reconnection to happen in seconds. For others, it is a ten-foot-wide concrete behemoth with an armed guard posted in front of it. Such a wall can feel insurmountable, impenetrable. But with each heartfelt apology, a chip is knocked out of the wall. And sometimes, a lot of chips must be knocked out to make an impact.

When she starts to feel, *Maybe he truly cares that he hurts me. Maybe if I show him this pain, he actually will care. Maybe he does care about me after all!*—this is when the magic of reconnection starts to happen, and the pain starts to subside. This is when couples start to turn it around. As a therapist, I live for these moments.

When it comes to communication, couples can really botch it. But this doesn't mean you should sit back and get complacent. Don't go home and tell your spouse, "Lori said it's okay I suck at communicating!" as you turn up the volume on the TV. Rather, seek comfort in the fact that with a little guidance and direction, you can learn to get back on track. You can learn to turn it around, too. And that learning has nothing to do with becoming an expert relationship communicator. It's simply about reconnecting over and over when you or your spouse has missed the boat.

As Dr. Sue Johnson—in my opinion, the most influential marriage counselor and researcher who ever lived— so eloquently said, "Love is a constant process of tuning in, connecting, missing and misreading cues, disconnecting, repairing, and finding deeper connection."[1] If you are unsure how to reconnect after you and your partner have botched everything, get out the highlighter and read on.

---

1. Johnson, Sue. *Love Sense: The Revolutionary New Science of Romantic Relationships.* New York: Little, Brown and Company, 2013.

Can't You See?
It's Hard for Everyone

I know when a marriage is doomed. It's true! It usually doesn't take long for me to tell when a marriage won't last. I just need to observe one simple truth about the couple. Once I've done that, I know that their marriage may not end today or tomorrow, but at some point, it will crumble—or at the very least, it will suffer deeply.

On the other hand, I also know when a relationship can thrive. It may be hard, and the road may look bleak, but I can see the light ahead, and it is good!

Now, I don't start thinking a marriage is doomed when I hear a spouse's long list of complaints about their partner, nor when I hear partners recount their struggles and frustrations in their marriage. I don't make that grim prediction when I hear how hard it is for them to balance their family life and their work life. I can't make it when I hear how exhausted they are and how this whole parenting-marriage-job gig is so freaking hard. I can't even make it when I see their tears over feeling so overwhelmed, inadequate, lonely, and sad. Nope—all this is to be expected, and most of us will experience these feelings and difficulties during this phase of life.

So what do I look for when I need to predict whether a marriage will succeed or fail? What is this magical key, this pivotal aspect that determines the fate of your relationship?

My chance to observe this most important truth about a couple—the defining moment in any therapy—comes right after I see a spouse share their sad, frustrating, exhausting, lonely experience. Will their partner show any semblance of an empathetic response—or not? Yes, friends—this magical, pivotal, defining feature of a healthy marriage, the feeling that *must* be present in both partners in order for a marriage to endure, the key to marital success is *empathy*.

Can the person sitting in front of me see anything outside their own experience? Can that person think—even for a split second—about how their partner may feel? Are they emotionally impacted when they learn what their partner thinks and experiences? And if they are, can they allow those emotions to influence their actions?

If not, well, I hate to say it, but the likelihood of saving that marriage is slim. Without empathy, a marriage will be on the road to Splitsville faster than your head can spin—or destined for an amount of fighting and feelings of loneliness I wouldn't wish on my worst enemy.

How Empathy Changes the Conversation

Amy and Joey came to therapy after eight years of marriage. At the time, they had a one- and a five-year-old. This was our conversation:

> Me: *How have things been going since our last session?*
>
> Amy *(miming quotation marks in the air with her*

fingers): Well, I'm just exhausted. Joey was "sick," and was basically boarded up in his room for four days, while I took care of not only all our kids' needs, but his, too!

Joey: I would have loved to join you guys in all the fun you were having. . . . I would have loved to go to the park and the children's museum. Except I felt horrible.

Amy: What I would give to be able to lay in bed for four days. That sounds amazing!

I hope you enjoyed your rest!

Joey: No, I didn't enjoy it! It was awful . . . and it would have been nice if you could understand that!

Amy: Oh, really?! It would have been nice if you could understand how exhausting it is for me to be a single parent and take care of you, too!

The hard part of empathy is that both partners often have valid points that would stand up in a court of law. It's easy to put empathy by the wayside and just use logic to defend your stance. Logically, you are probably right—but so is your spouse. Until one of them can tune in to the emotion involved, two people stuck on their own experiences will be at a standstill, with no hope of coming together.

Neither Amy nor Joey could get out of the logic of their arguments and into the other's emotions. Neither could allow himself or herself to be influenced by the feelings of the other. They were two people who cared a great deal about each other, with extremely valid needs, but with no chance of getting those needs met without empathy.

In my office, I watch the same fights go around and around when partners struggle with empathy. I have to give these spouses credit—they work incredibly hard to get their spouse's empathy. Unfortunately, they often use the same faulty methods, which usually wind up perpetuating a never-ending argument instead of invoking the empathetic response they long for.

I often see a stay-at-home mom desperately defend her role in the home. In an effort to get her husband's empathy, compassion and understanding, she recounts laundry lists of her never-ending chores and tells tales of tantrums and other horror stories of parenting. She thinks that if she paints the picture of how much she endures on a daily basis, he will surely see all she does. He will see how she has sacrificed pieces of her professional identify and self-care to pour herself into her family, and then he will empathize with her in the way she desperately needs and deserves. Once he empathizes with her, she knows he will naturally want to cheerlead her, shower her with appreciation, and even take care of her. Without hesitation, he will rub her feet, clean the kitchen, and give her a night off from putting the kids to bed, rescuing her from the endless monotony of parenting. No wonder she is fighting so hard for his empathy!

Meanwhile, I see the overworked husband desperately defend his role out of the home. I watch him vehemently explain the level of stress he is under at work and the intensity of his client's demands. I watch him defend his career and the effort he puts into his work as the sole reason they get to live in the nice house with the nice things. I watch him dismiss his wife's pleas for his help at home because his own work feels so stressful. He longs for her to see how he sacrifices his time and his hobbies and gives up his days on the golf course to coach his son's Little League team in his "spare time." He thinks that if he points out all this, she will empathize with him in the way he desperately needs and deserves. Once she empathizes with him, she will naturally want to show her appreciation, support his work endeavors, and give him a back massage after his tough day at work. Without hesitation, she will corral the kids into the other room to give him a moment of peace and quiet so that he can unwind after a hard day at work. No wonder he is fighting so hard for her empathy!

The problem is, as long as two people are defending their positions and not also putting themselves in the other's shoes, no one is getting their needs met.

Let me explain empathy as it pertains to marriage. My husband and I used to share all the financial contribution, household chores, daycare drop-offs, toilet paper pickups, etc. Then we suddenly moved across the country from Scottsdale, Arizona, to Charlotte, North Carolina. I was unable to practice immediately because I had to get my license transferred, and I got pregnant with baby number two. We went from being a financially comfortable two-income shared-chores family to being a one-provider and one-chore-doer family.

Other complications arose as well. When we originally started looking for houses in North Carolina, we had intended to find a move-in-ready home. Instead, we ended up in an abandoned home that still reeked of the neglect of its previous, divorcing couple—though we promised ourselves we'd renovate immediately. And even after we moved, our house in Scottsdale sat on the market for almost a year—so as our income dropped, our mortgage payment doubled.

Now, I'm no mathematician, but I'm pretty sure this put us in the red. And the predictable commission of my husband's previous sales territory was nowhere to be found, as he basically had to start over.

We barely saw each other. I was in a new city, with few friends, pregnant (three times, due to two miscarriages) and home alone with our two-year-old while my husband traveled all the time. He would come home late, exhausted and stressed beyond recognition. I had never seen him like this—he had been cruising on autopilot in his job since we got married. I had never experienced him as a stressed-out, overworked husband fearful for our financial future. And as is typical of most husbands, he was not particularly eloquent in communicating his level of stress, or his needs. For the first time in our marriage, we went to bed separately. He wanted to stay up and "unwind," while I was exhausted from chasing around our two-year-old and creating an entirely new human being in my own body.

This was the breeding ground for disconnection—the point where all good marriages go to die.

The lowest low that comes to mind is a memory of us yelling at each other over tiramisu during a date night, and riding home in silence. Inevitably, we started arguing again, and as we headed down our street to our house, in a moment of reactive hopelessness, I impulsively got out of the car and walked the rest of the way home.

Confession: Even marriage counselors lose their sh*% sometimes.

After this blowout, we were able to talk in the driveway and figure out a few things. I told him I was angry that we could not afford the renovations that we had originally planned for our new house. I told him that I was disappointed not because I was a superficial, materialistic, nothing's-ever-good-enough wife who needed a super luxurious, state-of-the-art home—but because I had expected one thing, and something else had happened. Because I wanted a home that made me feel good about having new people over to watch football games and have playdates. Because I wanted to make good friends and build a nice community for our family in our new city. It hadn't happened, and I was truly disappointed.

Now, as I listened to my husband talk in our dark driveway at what must have been almost midnight, I learned a few things, too. He told me that every time I criticized our spacious new '80s-inspired home, I criticized his ability to provide for us. In his mind, every time I complained that there were no pictures on the walls and that there was no money to buy any, I was saying he was basically worthless because he wasn't making enough money. And on top of that, he was seriously working his tail off. He was throwing himself into back-to-back meetings, long drives, late nights, and early mornings, worrying himself sick over our financial future during every sleepless night. And here I was, saying, "It's not good enough!"

I started to feel his pain. I even started to empathize with his position. I wondered what must it feel like to work that hard, to pour your heart and soul into something, and be told over and over that it wasn't enough?

Things changed for us after that. We stopped fighting about the house, and funnily enough, I actually stopped caring. I got patient, content and accepting of our humble abode. I actually even started to like our ceramic fruit backsplash, which became a fun conversation starter for new friends in our home. He also changed, in that whenever some extra income would come our way, he would forgo a golf outing or new golf clubs and encourage me to buy something new for the house. And our conversations began to change:

> *Me: How was your day?*
>
> *Chad: Well, my first appointment cancelled, and my second meeting was a total waste of time, but I actually had a good crowd for the dinner. I'm exhausted, though; I just got back to my hotel and it's ten p.m., and I need to get up by five thirty, because I have to drive two hours to get to my seven-thirty breakfast. How was your day?*
>
> *Me: Well, Brooklyn threw a huge fit and didn't take a nap. So she's pretty much been under my feet for thirteen straight hours, and I haven't had a break since six a.m.*
>
> *Chad: Gosh, that sucks. I don't know how you do it. I could never do that all day, every day. I would go nuts!*
>
> *Me: Me? I mean, she was nonstop, but I still got to go to the gym, meet up with friends at the park, and play in the backyard before her bedtime. What about you? You are working such long days, and having to start all over building clients. That's so stressful!*

Whose Day Is Tougher?

Even then, I reflected on our conversations and knew they were different than most. I knew this was a type of conversation that escaped many households, unfortunately. And I knew I couldn't get enough of my husband's validation as he told me that what I was doing was hard, and that he didn't know how I did it. I could have bathed in these words, I needed them so badly.

Now, typically, the conversations I hear between spouses in my office are not nearly so validating. Instead of empathetically responding to each other's struggles, I hear two people fiercely debating whose day was harder. Most often, I hear something like this:

> *Wife (to me): I am so sick of him getting home late and not making time for us. I do everything around here.*
>
> *Husband: Oh, right, and I do nothing. I guess I don't work sixty-plus hours a week to make sure we live in a nice house and the kids can go to gymnastics camp and you can get your new yoga pants and gym membership?*
>
> *Wife (to me): I'm sick of hearing about how I just sit around and eat bonbons all day. I just wish he could do what I do for one day. Just one day!*
>
> *And he would see how hard it is.*
>
> *Husband: Oh, I bet it is hard to go shopping and have playdates with your friends and pack a few lunches. Don't you get two free hours during nap time? I would love to have a two-hour break in my day!*
>
> *Wife: Well, aren't you one to talk—you get to ride in a car that doesn't smell like rotten milk or have Goldfish crackers smashed into the seats, while you go to a nice cushy job where you sit at a desk and sip your hot coffee and talk to other adults about things other than poop*

and nap times. I would kill to drink an entire cup of hot coffee without reheating it in the microwave three times. Three times I reheated it—and do you know what happened to it? It's still sitting in the microwave, because I forgot it when your son started screaming about losing his shoe as we were headed out the door!

Husband: Right, because that's what I do all day—sit around and drink coffee and talk about last night's epi-sode of The Walking Dead.

Wife: Well, at least you got to return some phone calls today, check some emails, read some news on the inter-net. Do you know the last time I watched something other than Paw Patrol *or* Peppa Pig*?*

Husband: It was your decision to stay home! You could go back to work any time you wanted. This was your decision, so I don't know why you complain about it all the time. If it's so bad, go back to work!

Wife: Is that what you want? You want to put our young kids in daycare all day long and pick them up at six p.m. and bring them home and put them to bed and never get to see them?

Husband: If it will make you stop complaining, then maybe I do!

People, please! Stop the madness! Can't you see? This is hard for everyone! Can't you see that you are *both* working hard and fighting huge, uphill battles and dealing with an abnormal, almost obscene amount of daily pressure to create a perfect life for your family? If you cannot see that, then it is time for a heart-to-heart. We need a *kumbaya* moment here. If you cannot empathize with your spouse and the pressures they are under—if you cannot see that your spouse is working hard to create a good life for your family, either inside or outside the home—then you have truly lost sight of how hard this phase of life is for both of you. Maybe your spouse isn't going about their day with the approach, attitude, and effectiveness you think are necessary; but they *are* doing the best they can. If you can see only how hard it is for you, and believe that you are the only burdened soul in this family while your spouse has it easy, then you are missing the boat. And it's a pretty big boat.

When you are lost and hopeless and do not know where to turn to figure out how to resolve a conflict, you can always turn to empathy. It works *every* time. Instead of bitter, resentful, spiteful conversations, you will have compassionate, caring, and comforting ones. When empathy is added, instead of stalemates and recurring fights, you will have two people leaning into each other, each excited to meet the needs of the other.

I actually feel extremely guilty about my ability to drop the kids off at the gym's childcare and go work out, or to meet a friend for coffee at ten a.m. while our kids are in preschool. It's silly. I think most moms of young children would tell me, "You deserve it! You will go crazy if you don't do something for yourself! It's better for you *and* your kids! It makes you a better mom!" I know this, and I don't hesitate to take a weekend girls' trip, or go out for a jog alone on a Saturday morning, when my husband is at home. But the guilt remains, because I know that he spends hours away, trying to churn up business to support our family, and I feel like I need to be in some sort of misery, too.

I am at the point that most of my friends have school-age kids. (Although I live in the South, I didn't start having kids until my mid-thirties, which makes me pretty much ancient.) I've noticed that during school hours, I often find it hard to reach said moms, because they are at a tennis clinic or their favorite Pilates class. Part of me cringes at this, not because I don't think they should do it—I do!—but because I really struggle with it myself. But this mentality has made me truly appreciate what my husband does for us, and how hard he works.

This goes both ways. I didn't feel guilty because my husband came home complaining and telling me how easy I had it when I wasn't working. It was quite the opposite: he told me I *should* meet up with friends or get a sitter once or twice a week, so that I could do some things for myself. He encouraged me to put our extremely hyperactive daughter in preschool three mornings a week, instead of two. I'm not sure if this was a chicken-or-egg problem—meaning I'm not sure if my appreciation of him caused him to be supportive of me, or vice versa. Most likely, it's a little bit of both. I've come to learn from my couples that patterns are quite cyclical. But instead of a crappy cycle wherein each of us argues that "what I do is harder!" or "what I do is more important," ours sounds more like, "'You work so hard for us.' 'No, you do.' 'No, you do!'" It's refreshing.

My empathy for the primary breadwinners of the world now runs deep. I truly cannot imagine taking that level of responsibility onto my shoulders. How stressful it would feel to have my family's financial future in my hands! How overwhelmed I would feel if I had to ensure I had adequate resources for my kids to go to college, have the weddings they desire, play in the sports leagues they want, attend the travel abroad programs or summer camps that will allow them to compete in this unforgiving world! I would likely collapse out of anxiety if I was burdened by all that pressure. I empathize for the breadwinners who feel they *have* to stay in an unfulfilling, overly demanding job because it gives their family the financial stability they desire. I can't imagine wrapping up work for the day with all this weight falling on my shoulders, only to come home and feel unappreciated, unwanted, or fussed at by the very people I am working so hard to take care of.

I also empathize with the stay-at-home dad. Stay-at-home dads are few and far between. To me, this means that those stay-at-home dads, who may have had to put aside their egos for the best interests of their family, are doing it alone. They are fighting stigmas and the potentially judgmental eyes of their career-obsessed friends, with a fraction (if any!) of the support available to the stay-at-home mom. The support that exists for moms has expanded in astounding ways in recent years. There are playgroups for every age, mommy meet-ups, mothers' mornings out, Mommy and Me programs—the list goes on and on. There is no question that the stay-at-home dad needs all this, too. But I have a hunch that support like this for dads is hard to find. They are doing the same job we moms do—the job we banter about endlessly on the playground, while getting validated by ten other moms who also felt like they were going to lose their minds by seven forty-five that morning. But those dads are doing it without the validation, support, and community that keeps most of us sane.

Empathy Begets Empathy

If you are a stay-at-home mom, you may have been thinking, "Nice for you! My husband would never support me or encourage me like that!" as I described my newly empathetic marriage above. Some thoughts on this. I wonder what would happen if he felt totally appreciated by you? I wonder what might happen if, instead of getting criticism when he gets home late, even though the food is burning and the kids are screaming, he was met with, "We are sooo glad you're here! Kids, Daddy's home! Yay!" I wonder what might happen if, instead of saying, "Well, dinner's burnt because you were twenty minutes late. I hope you like burnt pork chops," you said a short prayer at dinner, letting your kids see you thank God that your husband has a job and that there are pork chops on the table. Then you could proceed to tell him all about dealing with kid vomit, cleaning up dog poop, and getting punched in the face by your one-year-old. But if you want your spouse to come home ready to engage with you and the kids, you may want to consider whether he feels desired and valued when he sees you, or whether he feels criticized and inadequate instead. If he feels desired and valued, he will be more likely to support you, because he won't be so busy defending himself.

What I do not recommend is throwing boulder-sized insults at him the second he walks in the door, or becoming the world's best attorney and building a case for why your day was worse than his. I do recommend, however, having a real conversation, rooted in curiosity, about why he doesn't seem to value what you do.

Curiosity is one of my favorite tools. Instead of being accusatory (e.g. saying, "You don't value me!"), become curious.

You can say something like this:

> *You: Honey, I'm getting the sense that you feel what I do isn't important. Do you feel that way? Do you see my role at home as important?*

If he says he does, stay curious:

> *You: Then I wonder why I continue to feel like you don't? Can we try and figure this out? Because it means a lot to me to know that you value what I do for our family.*

And then, *listen!* You can even make sure he knows you care about his feelings, too, while remaining curious:

> *You: Do you feel that I value what you do for our family? Do you feel I appreciate you?*

And then listen some more! You might be amazed at what you learn if you are truly open, nondefensive, and inquisitive. You may actually learn how to turn this nasty cycle around. You may even start to empathize with him—*gasp!* And he may actually empathize with you—*astounding!* You may not resolve world hunger, and world peace may still be an issue, but for many couples, this type of conversation is transformational in their marriages.

Now, if curiosity falls flat, and your husband gives you a flippant response like "Of course I value you—now what's for dinner?"— then you may consider a more heartfelt approach. With my help, I've seen couples in my office do this exceptionally well. Here's how: Jessica and Chris had been together half their lives by the time they came to couples therapy. Chris had started a company, something he had always wanted to do. His business became a success around the time Jessica had their third child. After several years of putting her photography career on hold so she could act as the primary caregiver while Chris nurtured his business, Jessica experienced what she considered a pivotal moment. Chris had promised to get home at a certain time so that she could meet with one of her first clients in years as she tried to restart her career. Chris never showed. After calling him ten times and sending a barrage of text messages, Jessica had to cancel her plans.

When Chris realized his error, he called her to apologize. He also reminded her that he was the one who made the money, so while she was understandably upset, she needed to remember how important his job was for them.

Jessica started to fall into the same trap many of my other clients do. She wanted to yell at Chris and tell him how selfish, self-absorbed, and egotistical he was. She wanted to defend the importance of her work, which meant a lot to her even though it didn't pay the mortgage. However, with some gentle nudging from me, Jessica shifted out of defensiveness and blame and into her deeper emotions. With tears in her eyes, she simply looked at Chris and said, "When you do things that make me feel like your efforts are more valuable than mine, I get so sad. I long for you to see me as your equal. You are so important to me and this family; I just wish you could see me the same way. When it seems that you don't, it breaks my heart."

Chris said nothing for several seconds. I watched him process his wife's words—and then he seemed to melt as he said, "I'm so sorry; I never wanted you to feel like you are less than I am. I never want to see you this sad again." By the end of the session, I watched the color return to Jessica's face as they began to brainstorm ways to prioritize her work in their daily lives.

Now, husbands, this next part is for you. If your wife has read this and begun to try to understand you and talk to you in a less insulting, more heartfelt way, you need to respond to her, too. You need to understand the complicated web of factors influencing her as she tries to balance a job and family, or as she struggles with having taken the ultimate leap of deciding to go *all in* and make being a mom and wife her full-time job. It's time to display some empathy for her—not because she has asked you to, but because she just downright deserves it.

Husbands, if your wife works outside the home—full-time or part-time—and is in the position of balancing being Employee of the Year and Mom of the Year (because, let's face it, she is likely striving for perfection on both sides), you are in need of some serious empathy training. It may seem like I'm asking you to compare apples to apples—I mean, you are also balancing a full-time job with being a dad. What's the difference? I'm here to tell you there is a difference. The fact is, in American culture, it is usually the mom who must make the choice to sacrifice her career and sense of individual identity and stay home, or to split herself in two and continue her career while also being a mom. If she works, she will undoubtedly feel the pressure to be home with her children more often—pressure from her mom, her kids' teachers, her grandma, her neighbor, or the head of the PTA. No one is looking at her husband with those same judgmental eyes and saying, "Gosh, it must be so hard going to work every day and putting your child in daycare." No one is questioning his decision to work full-time. In fact, they fully expect him to work, stay late, travel, and basically move into his office during busy season. No one questions him—and if they do, they do not question him the way they would question his wife if she did the exact same thing.

So here sits your wife, who often feels like she is failing on both fronts. She is doing her best to stave off the mom-guilt she feels when she can't be at preschool for the Easter egg hunt, or can't be the one to pick up her kids from school and take them to soccer. When she does leave work early to volunteer at the school's bake sale because she has missed the last three years and remembers the judgmental stares of other moms, she feels guilty for leaving work when she notices the disappointed look on her boss's face. And worse, she hears the reports from her daughter or son at the kitchen table that *so-and-so's* mom was there for the school party—why wasn't she? No matter where she turns, she is letting someone down.

While she is spinning in this emotional turmoil, she is also constantly solving a logistical nightmare. She is playing the mind-spinning game of calculating how to get each kid to the right place at the right time, and relies on caregivers, friends, neighbors, classmates, and nannies to help. All the while, she is also seeing texts and emails of the plans her stay-at-home friends are making with their kids roll in daily. Or she may not even see this anymore, as they have stopped sending her the emails, knowing she can never make it.

The difference in her reality and yours, husband, is that she could name ten, twenty, a hundred friends and acquaintances who stay at home with their kids. There is always this other option. Whether it is a feasible option or not, it exists, and it's in the back of her mind all the time. She works her tail off to please her demanding boss, make the numbers to hit her bonus, and work overtime to please her clients; and she can't help thinking all the while: *Is this worth it?*

Then we have the courageous stay-at-home mom.

While I was staying home with my first daughter, I felt an overwhelming loss of identity. I used to engage daily in meaningful, sometimes life-changing conversations with other adults. Then I found myself on my knees, begging and pleading with my two-year-old: "Please, please poop in the potty! Mommy can't listen to you cry from constipation all day again! What will it take? Do you want candy, ice cream, a new iPad, a trip to Disney World, a million dollars? I'll do anything; just please poop in the potty!"

One of my friends always seemed to call when I was cleaning. When she asked me what I was doing, I would always tell her, "Oh, you know, just playing Cinderella!" which basically meant that I was forgoing all my training, education, gifts, and talents to clean my children's toilets.

And can we talk about the mom-guilt? We feel guilt all the time! We shouldn't be sitting down and taking this nap; we should be folding laundry, even though we are exhausted from being up three times last night dealing with our three-year-old's nightmares. We shouldn't let the children watch yet another show just so we can clean the house for the dinner guests we are hosting. We shouldn't just be sitting here, playing with our kids; we should be simultaneously multitasking and putting away dishes. And then we feel guilty that instead of fully engaging with our children, we are putting away dishes! It's insanity, and we do it all the time.

No matter if we stay at home or work part-time or full-time, this inner dialogue is constant. And the fear of falling behind and not parenting as well or providing the same number of opportunities for our kids as Cindy Lou does for her perfect twins down the street is overwhelming. We are constantly reading blogs, parenting books, and *Huffington Post* articles, and talking with fellow mom friends *ad nauseum*. Then our husbands come home and make a flippant comment about the kid's dirty face, and we want to erupt. Here's what you men don't understand: we obsess. We are consumed with thinking about our kids.

At one time, my husband and I traveled to Switzerland for his work. Our daughters were ten months and three years old at the time, and would be staying with my parents. It was my first time leaving the baby since I'd had her. In the weeks leading up to this trip, I lost so many nights of sleep, going over and over what needed to happen before I left and while I was gone. I was flooded with anxious thoughts, such as *Is she going to be okay? Am I the worst mom in the whole world for leaving her?!* I seriously—no joke—wrote a detailed ten-page, step-by-step, hour-by-hour manual for my parents on how to take care of my kids, all while my husband slept soundly beside me, dreaming of snowy Swiss mountaintops.

We are drowning in the desire to be good moms. We feel constant pressure to have perfectly behaved children in perfectly matching clothes in the perfect amount of preschool (not too much, or you get judged for being an absent mom; but not too little, or you are judged for being a helicopter mom) and the perfect number of extracurricular activities, while making sure they are going to be able to get into that perfect school.

Don't even get me started on the schools! The unbelievable amount of research that moms do—reading, touring, and talking to every mom friend in a twenty-mile radius—just to figure out schooling is mind-boggling. Then you, husband, come in and say, "You really are making too big of a deal about this school thing. Look at me—I went to my neighborhood school, and I turned out just fine." First of all, that is debatable. Second of all—*argh!*

Husbands, imagine you slaved over a project at work for three years, were consumed by it day in and day out—and then your boss said, "Well, looks like you could do better. Oh, and by the way, the work you are doing is not really a big deal to us. Actually, no need to stress about it, because it pretty much doesn't matter to us anyway." Husbands, you do not understand how, when we dropped off our tiny child at preschool for the first time, we sat in the parking lot and sobbed, and then proceeded to call three other mom friends so they could tell us that we hadn't caused them irreparable damage. All the while, you were at work, giving it absolutely no thought in the world—and then you came home and said, "Oh, yeah, today was her first day! How did it go?"

We are obsessed; we are consumed. Husbands, please understand: we need your validation, appreciation, support, and understanding; and we probably won't ask for it very nicely. That doesn't mean you get to check out and take a pass on this one. Your marriage may not survive if you do not get this.

Husbands, please ingrain these words into your head and your daily vocabulary, and see if your wife stops ripping your head off the second you walk in the door: "Wow, you have so many different things going on at once! My head would start to spin if I tried to do all that! It's amazing you keep it all straight!" Or, "I'm amazed everyone is still in one piece! Kids this age are so tough! And you are with them all day. Not only is everyone still in one piece, but you even managed to throw a casserole in the oven. I don't know how you do it!" Or, "We don't know what we would do without Mommy, do we, kids? She does so much for us. Let's all give her a hug and say thank you." I think you get the idea.

Empathy can have far-reaching effects. All the newfound empathy I have in my marriage has led me to a great appreciation for my husband and what he does for us. Naturally, I've therefore tried to teach our daughters to appreciate what their father does as well. Here's a conversation I had with my eldest daughter, then five years old, on the way to her school one day:

> *Me: Brooklyn, since I don't have to work today, we can go to the park after school. Isn't that great? Isn't it great that Daddy works so hard that I can stay home and play with you?*
>
> *Brooklyn: Mom, what happens if Daddy doesn't work hard?*
>
> *Me: Well, Brooklyn, he wouldn't make enough money for our house or our food or our clothes.*
>
> *Brooklyn: So we would have to live in a really small house?*
>
> *Me: Well, maybe. Yes, that could happen.*
>
> *Brooklyn: But we don't live in a really small house because Daddy makes lots of money? And people who live in small houses don't work hard, and they don't make lots of money?*
>
> *Me: Well—uh . . .*

This led to a whole new conversation about bragging and privacy. Anyway, my point is, you may be amazed at all that can happen when you start becoming empathetic. When it comes to relationship skills, empathy is in the top three. It's not necessarily something you are born with; rather, it is often something you learn and observe in others. If you need a little assistance in this area, start asking yourself these questions:

How does this situation make my spouse feel?

What is the hardest part of this for them?

What is it like to be in their shoes?

These simple questions can start to pave the road to more connecting conversations—and remember, empathy begets empathy. The more empathy you have, the more empathy he will have, and so on. You can never have too much of it.

Now, having empathy is not the same as giving your spouse a free pass, or making excuses for his poor behavior. Having empathy does not mean saying to yourself, "Well, I understand why he raged at me. He only yelled and threw a cup at me because he is so tired from work, and so stressed by his new promotion." No—that is called enabling, a topic on which I could write a whole different book. Having empathy means saying, "I wonder how what I'm doing impacts you. I wonder how you are taking my actions, my words, my gestures, my nonverbal cues. I truly wonder how that feels . . . for *you*."

Remember the fight I told you about at the beginning of this chapter, the one that consisted of my husband and me duking it out in the driveway at eleven o'clock at night? Well, a year later—seriously, a full year later—I was doing a Bible study that invited me to examine some of my marital regrets. This fight came to mind. Even though we were completely past it, and he never even hinted that there was any lingering hurt and anger on his part, I still had the desire in my heart to tell him I was wrong and that I was sorry.

So I did. And as I did, tears started to stream down my face—tears I hadn't even known I had. As I shared my apology, I was reminded of how much my words had hurt him a year ago, and I was sad.

He didn't need me to apologize, he told me gently. He was over it. But I could see in his eyes, and in the way he looked at me as I spoke, that I had touched him, and maybe even put out a tiny little fire of hurt and anger he didn't even know he had in him. And that, my friends, is empathy.

Women Are More
Critical Than Men

It is important for marriage counselors not to pick sides. We are supposed to remain neutral, reserving any judgment. But since this is a tell-all, here is my non-neutral, judgmental observation: women are more critical than men. Not just a little bit, but by a landslide.

If criticism were a sport in the Olympics, a woman would win gold every time. And silver and bronze, too. It's seriously our part-time job. We aren't happy in this moment, and you, husband, are the reason. We are stressed out and exhausted, and it's because you, husband, didn't do enough. You didn't help enough, in the exact way we needed, at the exact right time, with the exact right words and the exact right tone and facial expression. It's basically *all your fault!*

There, I said it. You, husband, are the cause of all my suffering and misfortune, so I must remind you of all your failings on a monthly, weekly, daily, and sometimes hourly basis. And to make matters even worse, you, husband, don't even care.

This is the point that lets you know that women criticizers everywhere have truly perfected the art of criticism: we dole out criticism *on top of* criticism. We say, "You, husband, are terrible because of what you did, and you are *really* terrible because of how you are handling it! And now that I have successfully stripped you of your sense of self-worth and manhood, can you please change your selfish, self-absorbed, immature ways and *get it right?!*" Now, if this doesn't motivate a person to change, I don't know what will.

Here is a fight I hear often:

> *Me (to wife): Have you told him how you feel?*
>
> *Wife: Yes. I've told him that he's selfish and only thinks about himself. He knows I hate it when he makes plans after work without asking me.*
>
> *Me (to husband): And what happens when she tells you these things?*
>
> *Husband: It's just one more thing. It's always something. I've stopped listening.*
>
> *Wife: See? He doesn't care!*
>
> *Me (internal thought):* No, it's not that he doesn't care. Actually, he has absolutely no hope, no expectation that if he did something different, you wouldn't find something wrong with that, too.

Here is another example:

> *Wife: He never compliments me. He never tells me I'm pretty, or that I look nice.*
>
> *Husband: You are pretty, and you do look nice today.*
>
> *Wife: You only said that because I asked you. You don't*

even mean it.

Husband: See? Even when I do it, it's not good enough!

Wife: Well, maybe if I didn't have to ask you for it, it would be!

I'll go ahead and tell you how this fight ends. She brings this up again in a few months and then reminds him that even though she told him in my office how she wanted his compliments, he still hasn't bothered to offer one up, "and it's been two months!"

Now, here's where she is missing the boat: she has no idea how her criticism on top of criticism scared the crap out of him when it comes to thinking about ever trying again. This is like a teacher standing at the front of the class on the first day of school and saying, "Students, here are all the books, essays, projects, and homework that you will have to do this year. Now, you can work as hard as you can, read the books, write the essays, create the projects, and attempt all the homework, but most likely, you will still get a D or an F. It's basically impossible to get an A. Actually, no one in my class ever has. And by the looks of you, I'm not feeling hopeful that you have what it takes either."

Once the teacher has done this, he can't turn around and say, "My students are terrible! They are lazy; they never do what I ask them; they sleep during class; and their homework is pathetic. I don't even know why I bother showing up to class, because I'm obviously the only one who cares about their education."

I know this sounds extreme and ridiculous, but this is what many—not all, but many—wives are feeling, when they first start coming to couples therapy. In their minds, they have tried everything, *everything*, to get through to their husbands, and nothing matters; nothing will make him change. They think he just doesn't care enough, or that he only cares about himself.

Is My Husband a Narcissist?

A small percentage of the male population qualify as narcissists. To the wives of each and every narcissist out there—I believe you, and you are in a terrible situation; and most likely, you want to run. But based on how most wives feel when they come to therapy, you would think that the vast majority of men are narcissists. According to their wives, they are self-absorbed, emotionless, selfish, and incapable of being vulnerable—and they surely don't care about their wives' needs.

I'm here to tell you that most of these men are not narcissistic. However, they may feel beaten down, defeated, deflated, and in some cases, completely emasculated. They can't even remember what it felt like to see a smile they created on your face. They can't remember the last time they heard you compliment their efforts or seem genuinely happy with the results of their actions. They can start to shift their focus, time, and energy onto things that give them good feelings, such as chasing the next work promotion—instead of spending that time and energy at home with the wife and kids.

This leads to the other most common fight:

> *Wife (no more than ten minutes after husband gets home): Seriously?! You're still checking your work emails? You never help me! All you care about is your precious work.*
>
> *Wife (to the children): Sorry, kids, we obviously aren't as important as Daddy's clients. Maybe if we pay him*

for his time like his clients do, he will actually pay attention to us.

The husband most likely says nothing at this point. If he is a fighter, he will shout back in anger, but often he just goes to his room, maybe even for the rest of the night. So she goes on:

> *Wife (yelling down the hallway as he shuts the door): I don't even know why you bother to come home. It's obvious where you want to be, and it's not like you are any help here anyway! You might as well just stay at work!*
>
> *Husband (internal thought):* I will next time.

And he often does. He continues to get home later and later, to put off the full-frontal assault he expects at home. She is left to believe that he gets home later and later because he cares less and less about her and the family. I find this fight to be one of the most common, tragic cycles couples face.

Recently, I was driving my husband to pick up his car in the shop. This is pretty much the only time I drive us anywhere, because he thinks I'm a terrible driver—which he proceeded to tell me during this short ride to the mechanic's.

The thing is, it's true: I *am* a bad driver. I got my new Toyota Highlander—the mom car you buy when you are resisting the minivan with every inch of your being, because you are hanging onto your pre-mom pride, even though you secretly know you would love the minivan and all the glory and comfort it has to offer—in January. I got into my first fender bender (my fault) in February, my second (my fault) later that same month, and my third (technically not my fault, but I still feel I may have had something to do with it) in March.

So I'm a bad driver. It's not really an opinion at this point, but more of a cold, hard fact. But even with this knowledge, I still felt the sting of my husband's criticism. He hadn't attacked my character or my personhood—just my driving. He was even right! I *am* a terrible driver! And I was still pissed and hurt! Why? Because even if there is truth to it, nothing digs deeper, hits a bigger chord, creates a greater wound, than hearing the person whose opinion means the most to you say something negative about you.

I shut down and remained quiet for the remainder of our car ride. He had no idea, and was humming along to the radio while I sulked in silence.

It wouldn't have mattered if my car insurance rep, Larry— who is now on my speed dial—said, "Ma'am, have you considered the fact that you are a terrible driver?" I would have said, "You're right, Larry, I *am* a terrible driver! Thank goodness I have good insurance! Now, where can I send you my thank-you note or fill out your glowing customer service report?" No, it only mattered so much because *my husband* had said it. I want my husband to think of me as an amazing, beautiful, extraordinary, even superhuman (at times) woman. It only mattered because I care so deeply what he thinks, above what anyone else does.

Now, when I tell *him* over and over how he did this and that wrong, that he failed me again and again, am I communicating to him how much his opinion matters to me, how much his view of me matters to me? *No!* I'm only communicating that I have extremely high expectations, and he has no chance in hell at meeting them—because, basically, he is a terrible human being.

Criticism from the person you love stings. Your husband values your opinion of him. He wants to know you see the good in him, even when he lets you down. He longs to know that even when he missteps and disappoints you, he is still the man you want to be with. And as long as he knows you value and love him, he will probably be able to handle your occasional frustrations with him.

Men: The Great Internalizers

Wives—our words matter, our words hurt, more than we can ever know. And the reason we often may never know is because our husbands internalize a lot of that hurt, and do not tell us.

We are not typically great internalizers, and are more likely to make the depths of our pain apparent—usually through telling our husbands how lousy they are for making us feel this way. Our husbands don't always do this. More often, they take it in and let it chip away at their sense of manhood until they start to feel like they do not have what it takes to make us happy.

When they start to feel this way, two things usually happen. First, they shut down and say nothing, which leads us to believe they truly don't care (*Ah-ha! I knew it! Just as I suspected!*) because they aren't saying or doing anything about it. And second, they stop trying. After all, what's the use? We're just going to criticize that, too. Nothing is ever enough, and they are exhausted by trying. Or maybe they are so sensitive to our words that they never even started.

Ladies—it is rare to find a husband in my office who does not view his wife's criticism as a message that he is "not good enough." Let me tell you what has happened when they get to the point of no longer trying: they have started believing they truly *aren't* good enough. And when they stop trying to make us happy, because they truly believe they can't, we cannot then turn around, pointing our raging fingers at anyone who will listen, and say, "See, he doesn't even *try* to make me happy! Don't you feel sorry for me? Shouldn't I get the Best Wife Award for putting up with this BS?!"

Aside from being expert criticizers, women are also exceptionally good at being totally blind to the impact of our criticism. We can be so blind to our husbands' pain.

I remember a young couple, married seven years, with two young children. During our session, she began explaining (often a fancy word for complaining) that her husband never opened up to her, never told her how he felt. She was upset about this. She wanted him to be more open with her. She wanted to feel emotionally connected to him.

It was within three breaths of this admission that she told me the running joke in their house was that she cared about the kids, and even the dog, more than him. He responded, "Yes, everything is more important than me." She laughed, and then continued on about how she was so frustrated that he never told her how he felt.

I told her, "It looks like he has told you exactly how he feels—he feels like everything is more important to you than he is."

As I said this, I saw that he had a very small tear in his eye. She stopped in her tracks when she saw the hurt look on his face, and said, "I mean, I knew he felt that way, but I didn't know it was a big deal."

Sometimes, I want to gently—or not so gently—shake my clients to get them to wake up. This was one of those moments.

I felt for this poor guy, who had been trying for years to tell his wife how unimportant he felt. Heck, her lack of care had even become the running family joke! "Ha ha! I don't care about you, husband! Ha ha! This four-legged animal that licks himself and poops in our backyard is more important than you! Isn't that hilarious?!"

We can be blind to our husbands' pain. They may not have the emotional vocabulary and ability to articulate their inner workings like us "expert women communicators." Their social and professional circles do not value the ability to do that well. But that does not give us the right to assume their emotions do not exist, or to tune in only if their feelings are communicated in a wonderfully vulnerable, articulate, and poetic way. That's never going to happen. So we have to be aware, catch the little comments, and notice the looks on their faces and the hurt in their eyes. We still have a responsibility to tune in—a responsibility to our husbands, to ourselves, and to our marriages.

I'm Not Criticizing—I Just Need Him to Change

A client once told me in a session, "I'm not criticizing him—I'm just telling him what he needs to change to make me happy!" She questioned me: "When he does something that upsets me, how am I supposed to let him know how I feel without telling him what he did wrong? I can't help it if he feels criticized—I have to be able to talk about the things that upset me. I can't control how that makes him feel."

I appreciated her argument. I even get stuck in that spot sometimes as a marriage counselor. I may watch a partner lament that her husband works too much, doesn't make time for her, left her to clean the kitchen without even offering to help, didn't help pick up the toys before guests came over, left his dirty laundry all over the floor, and expected her to pick it up. I hear all her gripes about how he did things wrong and she is upset. And there are times I buy right in. *Gosh,* I think, *he sounds terrible! How does she put up with him?*

The benefit of my job is that it gives me this expert insight—wisdom that comes from hearing spouses say the same things over and over in my office. I have the luxury of knowing that in spite of all his "failings," he desperately wants to please her. I know that despite his outward behaviors indicating that he doesn't give a damn about her, often he cares so much that it paralyzes him. Being privy to the private thoughts of these men during our sessions is truly the only way I could have learned this. I may be the only one to whom they have confessed, "It devastates me when I let her down," or "I get overwhelmed at times with how much it seems I disappoint her," or "I feel like I fail her all the time, which makes me feel like I'm a failure as a husband. It's the worst feeling in the world. It makes it hard to even try."

Because I know this, I tread lightly around my husband when I feel like he has let me down. Now, I've already confessed to communicating poorly at times. I acknowledge that I've been known to throw out a snarky, sarcastic comment when I feel he isn't pulling his weight. I admit that I can be insensitive to his feelings as I shout orders and demands when we have guests coming over for dinner. I'm sure I nag and carry on at times in a way that makes him want to put on his Bose headphones and tune me out. However, when the situation is a bit more significant than him ignoring the smell of our daughter's poopy diaper in the hope that I will change it before he has to, I try to be truly thoughtful in my approach.

One day, my husband came home to tell me about an amazing offer he received to play in a golf tournament in Bermuda. The tournament was scheduled over Memorial Day weekend, which would leave me and our daughters to participate in the weekend family festivities on our own. But as I heard him carry on like a giddy schoolboy who'd just gotten a kiss on the cheek from the girl of his dreams, I realized that despite the terrible timing of his request, I would oblige. We have a long history of being supportive of each other's hobbies and interests. He had supported me a million times, and I agreed to do the same for him.

He recognized, however, that this request was different. It would be an expensive trip, and his job security was on the rocks, which would leave our financial situation less than stable. And what was originally supposed to be a three-day excursion quickly turned into a five-day trip due to flight times and the tournament schedule. The original request, to which I'd agreed, had turned into something much greater.

I started to balk. I told him of my misgivings and concerns, and he reassured me it would all be fine. In my mind, I did everything short of cancelling his flight for him—yet he pressed on.

After he kissed me goodbye on the morning he left for the airport, I felt abandoned by him for the first time in our marriage. As he sent me beautiful pictures of paradise over the next four days, I continued to vacillate between feelings of sadness, jealousy, and anger.

I decided not to share these feelings with him until he returned, as I did not want to ruin his trip. (Yes, I know, I'm a saint.) As I thought about talking to him about my feelings, I thought about my strategy. I knew that if I came at him like an attack dog, he would feel like a big pile of dog sh*% and shut down.

I decided to proceed with caution. I could have so easily said, "How could you? You were so selfish! I can't believe you left us. I can't believe you made the decision to spend this holiday weekend away from your family. You knew how I felt about it, and you went anyway, because you do whatever it is you want to do!"

Instead, I said, "I didn't want to feel this way about your decision, but I do. For some reason, I felt so sad while you were away. I saw all my friends spending the weekend with their families, and I wanted to be with mine, too. I was angry because I had told you I thought this trip was a bad idea. I was angry that you didn't let my feelings influence your decision." Then I said, "I'm not telling you this because I want you to feel bad. Truly I don't. I am telling you this because it was hard for me, and I want to always let you know when I struggle."

As my husband responded with genuine apologies and proclamations that he realized he'd made the wrong decision, I continued to affirm him. I affirmed that my sadness had arisen because I missed him and wanted to be with him. I made sure he felt that my sadness was due to this desire to be with him, and not because he was a big fat failure. After hearing my hurt, he likely left our conversation feeling sad and disappointed—but he still felt loved and wanted.

Often, men who come to my office for counseling describe feeling sad and disappointed, too. However, they also describe feeling like scum of the earth. In those moments of criticism, they feel like they are the most hated person in their wives' eyes. I can scroll through my clients' words like a Rolodex and remember time after time that a husband has told me he shut down, pulled back, turned away, stormed out, and even left his marriage because he felt so hated by his wife.

I remember a husband and wife who came to me because he had decided to leave the marriage. She was devastated. In our session, she gently cried as she described how much she loved him, how much she wanted him to stay, how much she cared for him. As I looked to him to respond, I was shocked at the words that came out of his mouth. He said, "I had no idea she felt this way. By the way she has looked at me for the past ten years, I thought she basically hated me. I'm leaving because I just can't seem to be what she wants."

One of the hardest changes for a partner to make is learning how to ask for what they need without criticizing. It is so innate in us. "You didn't do it how I asked you to. You didn't do what I asked you to do. You didn't even think about what I need, did you? You aren't there for me when I need you. You aren't being helpful. You aren't listening to me. You aren't hearing me. You aren't understanding me. That's not how I told you to do it!" For many men, all they hear is, "You are a failure. You are a failure. You are a failure. You are a failure."

If you are interested in changing your approach, it helps to start with this question: What is it you need? Does he have to be home at exactly 6:04 every night, or do you just need to know that he's trying—trying to get back to you and the kids as soon as possible, while also balancing a tough boss or entitled clients, because he wants to be there for you, even when he sometimes fails? Do you really need him to pick up organic one-percent milk instead of generic, pesticide-filled, fatty whole milk? Or do you just need him to toss that crappy, lesser milk in the fridge, give you a hug, and say, "Man, I missed you. I was ready to leave work two hours ago, but I got caught up in things. So I ran through the grocery store and grabbed the first carton of milk I could find, so that I could get home to be with you and the kids."

There is a difference between needs and wants. Some couples spend 99 percent of their time arguing about wants, and totally miss the needs. If you only focus on what you want, you will often miss out on what you need. This is because, as you continue to rant and rave about what he didn't do that you wanted, he will start to feel so shut down, angry, and defeated that he can't possibly give you what you *really* need—connection, closeness, comfort, affection, appreciation, and support.

Start focusing on your needs in your conversations, instead of your wants. And be specific. Instead of saying, "I *want* you to be here when things get so crazy in the evenings, when I'm struggling with bedtimes and temper tantrums over toothbrushes and messy dishes," try, "I *need* to know you are in this with me, even if you're not right here." Instead of saying, "I *want* you to anticipate that I had a crappy day and didn't feel like making dinner, and bring home a pizza," try, "I *need* to know we are on the same team, and that you support me and the decision I made to give the kids macaroni and cheese for the third night in a row." Instead of saying, "I *want* you to start planning my birthday celebration three months ahead of time and create a super thoughtful picture book of our favorite times together, coupled with that Kendra Scott necklace I've been hinting at," try, "I *need* to know that you love me and that I'm important, whether or not you had time in our busy lives to make an elaborate plan for my upcoming birthday."

It helps to think about what you need, instead of how he didn't do things the way you wanted. Instead, remember a time he got it right—a time when you did feel loved, supported, and cared for by him. Remind him of those times, and of how much it helped when he did those things, said those things, and acted in those ways. And even though you know life is crazy and busy, when he stops for even one second to give you a hug, kiss your forehead, and tell you that you are doing a good job, take the time to tell him that his efforts work. That they work every time, because they came from him. Because when a man feels like he has a chance in hell of getting it right, he might actually start trying.

Happy Couples Hurt Each Other All the Time

I used to love it when my single friends came to me for dating advice after I became a marriage counselor. They would rattle off their lists of concerns about their new relationships, and I would let them know whether or not I thought their concerns were deal breakers. Our conversations usually went something like this:

> *Dating friend: He didn't even call me to ask to go out until two hours before he wanted to go. Doesn't he know I don't sit around just waiting for him? It's so disrespectful!*
>
> *Me: No biggie. What else?*
>
> *Dating friend: And he hates to do anything after work on Fridays, so I have to tiptoe around his "need for downtime" when making any plans. It's so annoying.*
>
> *Me: No red flags there. What else?*
>
> *Dating friend: He always insists I go to his place. I think it's ridiculous and unfair that I'm the one who*

has to make the sacrifice. It almost seems like he doesn't want to be inconvenienced in any way for me. I'm starting to feel pretty hurt about it.

Me: What happens when you tell him you are hurt?

Dating friend: Oh, he totally freaks out. And wants to shut down the conversation immediately. I don't even bring it up now.

Me: Ugh, now that could be a problem.

Couples spend hundreds of dollars in therapy, and do you know what they are doing most of the time? Figuring out how to talk about hurts. For some, it's figuring out how to share hurts in a way that doesn't leave their partner heading for the hills. For others, it's gaining the courage to show even a hint of their hurt without getting shot down by their partner or looking "weak."

I would love to save you money. Spend that on a nice Hawaiian vacation (that is probably long overdue).

Learn how to share your hurts. Learn how to hear your partner's hurts. Because here's the cold, hard truth: happy couples hurt each other all the time. You may be sitting at a restaurant, looking over at the laughing couple gazing in each other's eyes, and thinking, *I bet he never makes her feel bad.* Yes, he does. He may not know he is doing it; he may even have a heart made of pure gold—but he still hurts her on occasion, even if he doesn't mean to. The secret to their happiness, however, is likely that he knows how to talk about it when the inevitable hurts happen.

Now, I didn't say he knows how to fix it. He surely does not. He does not know how to learn from all his previous mistakes, brainstorm, and flawlessly adapt to all he has learned about what hurts her. What he has done is simply learn how to talk about it, how to hear it, and how to make sure she still knows he loves and thinks of her, even if he sometimes acts like he doesn't.

What If My Spouse Doesn't Care About My Hurts?

Learn how to share your hurts, and do it early on. The longer you wait, the bigger the hurts, the deeper the pain, and the more complex everything will become.

Erin and Jonathan had been married for twenty-five years and had two kids when they came to therapy. In typical fighting-couple fashion, Erin explained that she had been hurt by Jonathan over and over again, and that he didn't even care. And man, did it seem like she was right. I mean, this guy didn't blink an eye. She wept, and he stared. I poked and prodded at him, and—nothing. I asked him how her sobs made him feel, and he just shrugged. I started to fear that he had indeed emotionally checked out of this relationship, to the point that he didn't even care that she was hurting.

But after several sessions like this, Jonathan finally cracked. He began to cry. His lip quivered, his hands were shaky, and his face softened. I asked him what was happening, and he said, "I have hurt her for so long, in so many ways, I can't possibly imagine that there is anything I can do for her now. It's too big at this point, too much, too overwhelming. I feel like I've dug myself so far into a hole, I cannot possibly get out. I fear there is no way I can make this better for her." Now, does that sound like someone who doesn't care?

cs

Another couple, Logan and Ashley, came to me on the brink of total collapse. They had been together for eight years and had two kids. We reviewed the questionnaire Logan had completed for the first session. He shyly shared his concerns about the marriage, stating that Ashley didn't care about how he felt. I asked him more about this, and he revealed to me what he'd written on his form. Where he was supposed to rank the problem on a scale of one to ten, he had written down one thing in big fat letters. It said, "She doesn't care about me," and next to that, "100%." I asked him what that meant, and he said it meant that he felt she didn't care about him, one hundred percent of the time. Ouch!

I asked him, "How do you let her know this is how you feel?"

And he said, "I don't."

What?! You don't tell her? I can't seem to restrain myself from telling my husband when he *sneezes* in a way that hurts my feelings. And you never happen to mention or allude to the fact that the person with whom you have chosen to spend the rest of your life, have kids, buy a house and grow old, cares *nothing* about you?

In these moments, my heart simultaneously breaks and fills up with hope. It breaks because couples carry these deep hurts for years and years without even so much as hinting at the depths of their pain. But at the same time, the fact that they have trusted me, and each other, enough to put even a little piece of this pain out in the open lets me know there is hope for the marriage yet. They are at least willing to share their hurts, show their vulnerabilities, and open themselves up to yet more pain. Because the truth is, the only thing more painful than feeling deeply hurt by your spouse is to tell them so and see them respond in a way that makes you feel like they don't care. The amount of fear that this possibility instills in couples will often paralyze them into saying nothing at all, sometimes for years and years. These unexpressed hurts are like poison in a marriage. They infiltrate everything—every comment, every facial expression, every joke, and every touch. This is why, in a healthy relationship, there *has* to be a way to talk about hurts.

My favorite couples are the young couples, still dating, or perhaps newly engaged, who want to start things off on the right path. I just want to hug these couples and cheer them on with huge signs and pom-poms, and say, "Good for you! Good for you for being so proactive and not waiting years and years to learn how to do this whole relationship thing! Good for you for tackling this head-on!"

Many of my clients excel professionally. They are CEOs, doctors, attorneys, or heads of departments managing hundreds of people. They win professional awards, receive promotions and bonuses, are featured in business journals, and attend dinners with titles like "Charlotte's 40 Under 40." As a result, they often come to me frustrated by one thing: it is baffling, mind-boggling to them that they can achieve so much professional success while failing so miserably in their marriages. They cannot understand why they have been able to figure out complex, intricate, almost impossible problems with multiple moving parts in their work, but cannot seem to figure out how to make their spouses happy.

There are good reasons for this. First of all, most of these people did not have proper role models when they were growing up. Often, their parents had even more severely dysfunctional relationships, acting as good examples of everything *not* to do, rather than as good examples of healthy couples. Second, many of my clients never learned what they *should* do. Unlike their professions, in which they have spent hours, years, and decades learning, training, being mentored, and receiving degrees and certifications and doctorates, they have often spent less than five minutes thinking about what type of spouse they want to be and how they might achieve this. I've already started asking my children what they want to be when they grow up—a question that consumes the mind of almost every young adult. But no one— seriously no one—is usually asked, or asks themselves, "What kind of spouse do I want to be?" We sure as heck do not take any classes named "Successful Relationships 101" in high school, college, or graduate school.

The truth is, you don't know how to be a good spouse, because you were never taught. But I have some good news: there is no time like the present to start learning.

One of the worst reasons someone can come to marriage counseling is to change their spouse. However, this is consistently one of the most compelling reasons that motivates couples to come in.

I need to confess something: I can't change your spouse. I often tell my clients, "I'm pretty good. I've helped couples overcome even the most hopeless and loveless marriages. But I'm not a magician. I have no magic wand. I can't change your spouse."

I will not be surprised when my schedule starts to look very bleak after revealing this therapists' secret. What *can* change, however, is the way you talk to each other, the conversations you have, and the way you let each other know you are hurting. And changing this changes everything.

I Tell My Spouse My Hurts, But Nothing Changes

This is a harsh reality about marriage: you are going to hurt each other's feelings. Not just a little bit, not just once in a while, but often and frequently, and without even knowing it. Actually, most often, you would have never in a million years thought that the thing you did or said hurt your spouse's feelings. *That? That hurt your feelings? Really?* Yes, it did. And while we are at it, so did *this*, and *this*, and *that*.

Some of you may be thinking, *I tell him how much he hurts me all the time! But nothing changes! He just keeps doing it again and again. I don't even bother wasting my breath anymore.* This is a knock-me-over-the-head sign that intervention may be necessary. If you have stopped even bringing up your hurts because it feels like they fall on deaf ears, start using some of the strategies in this chapter. And if that still doesn't seem to work, let someone help you.

I have already confessed that my husband and I have pretty poor communication at times, and repeat some of the same silly arguments over and over again. Over the course of our marriage, I have probably asked him five thousand times to please, please put all the food down the trash disposal when he puts his dishes in the sink. When he doesn't, the smell that hits me when I come downstairs the next morning is nauseating. (Especially when I was pregnant—I would literally sprint to the nearest bathroom, gagging.) But this will never change, and I have accepted that. I still tell him to run the disposal, but I have absolutely no hope that he will ever start to do as I ask. It's a good thing for my husband that his leaving food in the kitchen sink does not happen to be a deal breaker for me.

We all have things we wish our spouses would do differently. Some may be annoying, frustrating, or downright infuriating at times. If they aren't deal breakers, you can reserve the right to decide whether voicing your concerns is worth the precious breath in your lungs. But if your spouse acts in ways that hurt you or make you feel unimportant, unappreciated, unsupported, unloved, or uncared for, you *have* to have a way to talk about this.

I love it when couples share the unsolvable nature of their conflicts with me:

> *Me: Have you talked about it together?*
>
> *Wife: It's pointless. Nothing ever gets resolved, and he never listens anyway.*
>
> *Me: Can you tell me a little bit about these conversations?*
>
> *Wife: Well, I told him he is such a jerk when he yells at me, and he told me he wouldn't yell at me if I wasn't on his case all the time. And then I told him I wouldn't be on his case all the time if he would actually listen to me and do the things I tell him to do. And then he said maybe he would listen to me if I weren't carrying on like an ungrateful, nagging wife. See?! It's unresolvable! There's no way to get through to him!*

There is, and it would be helpful if it didn't involve yelling, screaming, demanding, accusing, questioning, criticizing, attacking, or debating. Now, I stick to my original stance that communication does not have to look perfect in these moments. It doesn't. But typically, spouses react so strongly only when so many unresolved hurts have built up—hurt on top of hurt—that they are raw. Like the skin of a burn victim, they are so wounded, so open, that even the slightest touch—even the *hint* of a slight touch—can feel incredibly painful, and ignite harsh feelings.

This is why it's so important to address hurts early and often;

and if you come at your spouse sounding like a raging, ranting lunatic, apologize. Then try again later, when you are calm—and if necessary, as part of a therapy session with a skilled marriage counselor.

Let's use the conversation above to demonstrate a more effective approach:

> *Wife (to me): He just gets so mad, I don't think I can take it anymore. His anger is unpredictable and hurtful; I'm sick of it.*
>
> *Me (to wife): Can you talk to him about what happens for you emotionally when he yells at you?*
>
> *Wife (to husband): When you yell at me, it's awful for me. In that moment, it feels like you hate me, that you are so disappointed in me. It reminds me of the way my dad used to yell at me, and I would run into my room and hide.*
>
> *Me (to wife): Can you share with him what happens when you are reminded of how your dad would yell at you?*
>
> *Wife (to husband): My heart starts to race, my body gets tense, and I start to feel anxious. Even worthless. Like I have let you down to the point that you don't even love me. I start to feel like you are so angry with me, so disappointed in me, that you don't want me anymore.*
>
> *Husband (to wife): You start to think I could leave you in those moments?*

Wife: Sometimes I do. I know it sounds silly, but it just seems like I make you so angry. Why do you think I get so emotional and cry?

Husband: I just figured you overreact because you've had a bad day or something. I didn't know it gets that scary for you.

Wife: It does—because I love you so much. I care about you so much. That's why I get so emotional in those moments.

Husband (to me): I mean, I knew she didn't like my yelling, but I didn't think it was this painful for her.

Me (to husband): Can you tell her what it's like for you to hear how painful this is for her?

Husband (to wife, with tears in his eyes): I feel stupid. And sad. I didn't get how much my anger hurt you. I never want to make you feel that way again. I'm really sorry.

Wife (to me): I want to believe him; I want to trust him, but I'm afraid he's just going to do it again.

And he probably will. He may not yet know how to keep from yelling at you when he feels angry or agitated, but now he actually wants to know. He's actually motivated to learn. He wants to learn how to control himself in those moments so that it doesn't hurt you so much. And as you keep sharing how much his words hurt—because of your love for him, not because he is an angry asshole—he will keep listening and tweaking and listening and tweaking.

These types of conversations often have to play out many times before a couple's response patterns start to shift. That's right: even happy couples hurt each other, in the same ways, over and over again—and they have to talk about it again and again. The difference is that the hurts become milder, their conversations shorter and less intense, and they regain ground quicker. These fights don't turn into blowouts or three days of not talking to each other. They happen, the couple talks about it, and they move on. They can do this because they know how to say the following things:

> *This thing you did hurt me . . .*
>
> *. . . and it hurt me because I care about you so much.*
>
> *It made me feel like I wasn't important to you, which hurts me, because you are very important to me.*
>
> *I think I just need to understand why you did it, and to know that you do care about me, that I am important to you. Because that matters more to me than anything in the world.*

And then they say:

> *Thank you! Thank you for hearing my hurts, for letting me tell you about them. When you do that, I do feel that you care about me, that I am important to you—so thank you.*

Having the Ears to Hear

Now, you can't just dole it out and not learn how to take it. You have to be able to listen to your spouse when they talk about their hurts.

There are two major pitfalls when it comes to hearing hurts. The first is the moment that, having shared their pain, a hurting spouse is immediately met with, "Now you know how I feel." This response makes me want to take a flyswatter and smack the responding spouse on the back of the hand.

I admit, I say this too—especially when my husband has had the kids by himself for all of three minutes, and starts to complain. In those moments, I want to scream from the mountaintops with a megaphone: "NOW YOU KNOW HOW I FEEL ALL THE TIME!" But there is nothing that shuts down communication faster than saying, "Now you know how I feel!" whenever your spouse actually expresses a feeling.

Here is the other major pitfall. I heard this quote from two spouses in two separate therapy sessions one day: "I want him to be able to talk about it, to tell me how he feels." And so he does. He tells her that he feels hurt over something that happened— and she says, "That just makes me so mad to hear that!"

You have to have the ears to hear your spouse's hurts. For some people, this is extremely difficult. They get too reactive, defensive, or wrapped up in their own shame to hear their partner's pain. When they hear their partner's hurt, there is a part of them that feels like a failure, inadequate, a disappointment. We call this shame. This shame leads to reactions born of anger ("What is wrong with you!?"), defensiveness ("Well, I wouldn't have done that if you hadn't done this!" or "What about what you did?!"), and shutdown filled with inner turmoil ("I'm a failure.

I'm not capable of making my partner happy."). If these are your go-to responses, you may benefit from a marriage counselor, who can help you manage that reactivity so that you can hear your partner and be there for them when they are in pain.

Most spouses have an extremely hard time understanding this crucial truth about hurts in relationships: you can be the one to make them feel better, even when you are the one that caused their pain! Read that again. Let it sink in. There is actually *no one else in the world* that can comfort your spouse better than you in those moments. I know this is confusing; it seems backward, and it doesn't make any sense. "Why would you want me to comfort you? I'm the one who hurt you." But the truth is, your spouse *does* want that, and desperately.

I remember a couple, Brian and Madison, who shared in their couples session the story of their most recent fight. They had been to a work party with Brian's coworkers. Madison had felt anxious about being at the party without people she knew. She shared her fear with Brian, and he promised he would stay by her side—but he didn't. And when she finally found him on the other side of the party, he was talking to another woman.

During our session, Brian wanted to explain that the conversation had been innocent. He wasn't flirting; this was just an example of his wife being insecure and controlling, "like she always is." After coaching and listening and more coaching and listening, he finally let his guard down to hear her. To hear how, in that moment, she feared that he had forgotten her—that he cared more about this random woman than he cared about her. She felt rejected, and scared that he no longer wanted her.

After he was able to share with her how deeply he felt her pain and how sorry he was to have let her down, I asked him how he felt. He responded, "Relieved." He was relieved that he had been able to say, "I did that to you. I can see how that hurt you badly. It hurts me to see how I hurt you, and I'm sorry."

And an amazing thing happened: his words actually worked. His previously fuming wife leaned in and said, "I don't feel angry anymore. I just feel connected."

There is a huge lesson we can learn from this conversation: absolutely *nothing* got "fixed." There were no grand solutions, no figuring out who was *really* to blame. Was she too sensitive and insecure? Was he self-absorbed and inappropriate? We didn't take a poll or survey or bring out the grand jury. There were no promises of what they would do next time, or ideas offered on how to prevent this from *ever happening again!* She didn't need that. She just needed to hear, "I see that I hurt you, I'm sad that I hurt you, and I'm sorry."

You wouldn't believe how many sessions and how much coaching it takes to get couples to finally utter these simple words. So save yourself some time, money, and frustration. Learn these words. Learn them now, and practice them. Say them out loud to your mirror as you get ready in the morning. Put them on a Post-it Note on your rearview mirror. Make it a point to learn how to hear you partner's pain, and if you can't, have someone help you.

In my office, I listen to people's pain all day long. There is a lot of pain present when a marriage is on the rocks. Therefore, I spend most of my working life helping people find comfort in their pain. I spend more time soothing pain than most people spend doing their laundry. I'm kind of a pro by now, to be honest—and I've learned that the reason I'm so good at it is because I'm not the one that caused the pain. Therefore, it's easy for me to lean in and listen. It's automatic to offer validation, understanding, and loads of empathy to my clients as they share the depths of their hurt. I don't have an ounce of defensiveness in me as they sob about their pain, because I didn't have an ounce of responsibility in creating it.

When my five-year-old daughter first joined the swim team, she was so excited for her daily swim practice. After a few days, however, she began to complain of water in her ears. A more seasoned swim-mom told me that eardrops with alcohol in them would absorb the water. *Sounds good to me,* I thought.

My daughter and I stopped at CVS after swim practice and bought the drops. Seeing no reason to delay, we opened the packaging in the car, still parked in the CVS parking lot, and applied a drop to her ear.

Words can't describe the level of freak-out that ensued. My daughter screamed in ways that made me sure the police would be knocking on my window in seconds. After she finally started to calm down, she looked at me with betrayal in her eyes and cried, "What did you put in my ears?! Are you sure you did it right? Did you read the package? Did you buy the right drops?" "I think so," I replied with hesitation.

The next day, we went to the pediatrician, who diagnosed her with severe swimmer's ear. As I recounted the traumatic scene that had unfolded the night before, the doctor explained that in giving my daughter eardrops, I had essentially poured alcohol on an open wound. "Yep," she said, "that really hurts." She wrote me a prescription for the correct drops.

I apologized profusely to my daughter for causing her pain. I even lost a bit of sleep the next few nights, feeling so guilty that I had made that honest mistake. I put it on my lengthening list of mom-guilts.

A few weeks later, my daughter got pink eye. She is prone to it, and we still had drops from when she had gotten it before. I took them out of the medicine cabinet and said, "Here you go, Brooklyn; we just need to put a few drops in your eyes." Naturally, she resisted, and the next forty-five minutes were a flashback to that fateful day in the CVS parking lot. As Brooklyn cried and cried, my patience wore thinner and thinner. I knew why she was crying. I knew the experience had scarred her, and the thought of any drops anywhere near her brought back her memories of the pain she had endured. I struggled to hear her cries for the same reason: they reminded me of the pain I had caused when I gave her the wrong medicine. They reminded me of how I had hurt her—and the guilt came rushing back.

As the mom-guilt flooded me, I wanted so badly for her cries to stop—because then, my guilt would stop. I wanted so badly to say, "Brooklyn, chill out! This isn't a big deal! It's just a few drops; calm down!" But there was also a wise voice in my head, saying, "Be patient with her. She is scared; she is uncertain; she is unsure. You need to be gentle, patient, loving, and comforting."

I will be honest: my guilty voice outweighed my comforting voice, and I told her many times, "Just calm down already!" I'll be the first to admit that it is really, really hard to confront the pain you have caused—even for a pro comforter.

My Spouse Won't Let Things Go

You may be reading this and thinking, *I do hear her hurts. I do listen, but she just keeps going on and on and on about it. I don't know how much more I can take.*

A few thoughts on this. In order to move on, the person who was hurt must be able to make sense of what happened. They have to understand it.

I used to get this wrong. I remember a friend coming to me because her husband could not let go of the fact that she had broken up with him when they were dating. Even though they ended up together, got married, and had children, he was still plagued by the memory, and would bring it up often. I remember telling her, "He just needs to get over this! He decided to marry you with this knowledge, and he needs to let it go."

I was wrong. I admit it. The truth is, he couldn't let it go, because he still couldn't understand it. He couldn't make sense of how that had happened. Why had she left him? Why had she wanted him back? If a spouse can't make sense of something, they can't feel confident that it won't happen again. As a result, they stay anxious, scared, and often accusatory. They need your help— which means you have to understand why it happened, too.

Often, these hurt spouses will go to friends or family to seek counsel. They will hear theories and hypotheses about why you did what you did. The problem is, these guesses will not comfort them in the midst of a panic attack, when they become fearful that this could happen again. What *does* comfort them is hearing from you that you understand why you did this thing. They need to hear your best guess, based on lots of reflection, consultation, and analysis. And they also need to hear what you are *going* to do, your plan to make sure you don't get to that place again—because the last thing you would ever want to do is hurt them that way again.

Some of you are thinking, *I did that, too! I apologized genuinely, I understand how it happened, my spouse understands how it happened, and they* still *won't let it go!*

I get it. Sometimes I get sick of hearing about my husband's pain, too. Everyone has their limits. I remember when we had just moved into our new neighborhood in our new city, and my husband joined the neighborhood softball team. My husband did not know a single person on this team, but he is a great softball player, and the team was excited about their stellar new teammate. During their first game, he stepped up to the plate and swung his bat like he had done a million times before, always with crowd-pleasing results—and he missed. He probably hadn't missed a pitch since middle school. And then a truly tragic thing happened. The pitcher tossed another pitch—and he missed again.

Now, this may not sound like a big deal to most, but to my supercompetitive, let's-see-who-can-run-the-fastest-to-the-fence-or-hike-up-the-hill-first husband, this was potentially life-ending. I cannot express how much he sulked and stewed over this. At first, I listened, as a good, empathetic, supportive wife and marriage counselor should. "Oh, no, I know that was so hard for you! I'm so sorry this happened! What can I do to help? Can I rub your feet? Get you a cold beer? I'm sure they know you just had an off night. I'm sure next time will be great, and you will redeem yourself."

But over the next few days, as he continued to brood, my empathy and patience got pretty much shot. I mean, let's be honest—we weren't talking about lost lives, terminal illnesses, or financial ruin. We were talking about a silly little softball game played by a bunch of forty-year-old men who were going to complain for the entire next day about their sore muscles and the fact that they didn't have the stamina they used to out there. I had reached my limit. I was done listening.

I say this to empathize with you supportive, persistent, patient spouses who are doing your best to provide the type of comfort that will finally allow your dear, sweet husband or wife to *finally move on, already!* I realize you may have your limits, too. It may be time to get honest. It may be time to tell your beloved, pained partner, as gently as possible, "I care so much about your hurts, I want so badly to make this better for you, and I feel like I'm not. And I'm starting to burn out. It's not that I think you should already be over this, because everything takes time, and who am I to judge how much time this will take for you? But I'm losing steam, and I may need some direction, some guidance, or maybe even a short break from talking about it. I just don't want to burn out completely and have you stop feeling safe in coming to me. I always want to be able to be there for you."

Find a way to talk about hurts. And do it until you can't possibly do it anymore.

There is one final issue I want you to consider when trying to resolve the hurts in your marriage. If you feel like you are going over and over the same hurts and it doesn't seem to make them better, or if your spouse doesn't seem to be letting them go, consider that the dynamic between you may need tweaking. Often, the very difficulties between spouses that created the hurt in the first place also makes it difficult to resolve. For example, one partner may bring things up in a heated fashion, and the other will shut down. Or both of you may avoid bringing up issues altogether, in an effort to keep the peace at all costs. These types of dynamics may have happened on a smaller scale countless times in your marriage, but ignite when a bigger hurt rears its head.

These dynamics can make resolving hurts in your marriage very tricky. I will talk in later chapters about how to address some of them, so stayed tuned if this sounds like it may be happening to you.

I also want to offer some encouragement. If you or your

spouse is reeling from the hurts in your marriage, remember: the pain that comes from hurt provides an amazing opportunity for connection. Going through a marriage on autopilot, without navigating the natural hurts that arise when two people make a life together, does not create intimacy. It is the navigation of these hurts, the sharing of yours with your spouse and the learning about theirs, that creates the kind of intimacy that bonds two people for life. The next time you see pain in your spouse, instead of thinking, *Ugh, here we go again,* or panicking and assuming you have failed your spouse again, I encourage you to acknowledge the opportunity before you—the opportunity to lean in and learn about your spouse, learn about their pain, and learn what helps. Then you can join the droves of healthy couples who strengthen their marriages with every hurt, using those hurts and their pain to connect in deeper ways.

Pain either connects or divides people. Your attitude toward your pain can make all the difference when it comes to the direction in which it takes your marriage.

Your Spouse Is Incapable

Many of you are thinking, *Ah-ha! I knew it! I knew my spouse was incapable; that's what I was trying to tell you! That's why our marriage is falling apart!*

No. Let me finish. Your spouse is incapable of being your everything. I may or may not have closed my eyes and belted out "Everything I Do, I Do It for You" by Bryan Adams circa 1990 as I drove down the road in my super-sweet Mazda 626 hatchback. But the truth is, even though I love my husband, everything I do is not for him. And everything he does should not be for me.

I hate to be the one to burst the bubble of all you hopeless romantics out there, but your spouse cannot and should not be equipped to make you completely happy. And they shouldn't have all their eggs in your basket, either. You and your spouse will fail every time.

There has to be a balance between your life with your spouse and your life without them. That balance is different in every marriage, but you need to find it. Together.

When I was pregnant with my second daughter, I hit a level of exhaustion and fatigue that gave me a glimpse of why sleep deprivation is used as a method of torture. My super-active two-year-old was almost the death of me, getting out of her bed thirty times a night, seven nights in a row. My husband would come home from work and find me zombielike, in a fetal position, practically begging for a merciful death. I had lost all patience, and most of my mind.

One day, my husband told me that he had finally gotten to sign up for some volunteer work he had been wanting to do. He would be mentoring a seven-year-old kid, Jack, in math at a Title I school. He was excited to be going to the school early on Friday mornings to offer his help and mathematical expertise to this young lad.

I did not take this well. In fact, I had a complete meltdown, during which I told my husband that there was no way in hell that this "Jack" could possibly, even on his worst day, need him in the way I needed my husband right now.

Later, when I was a bit more caught up on sleep, I felt like the worst person in the world for shaming my husband as he tried to do something so generous. I should probably write Jack an apologetic note for attempting to interfere with his education.

It's hard to find that balance.

How to Support Life Outside Your Marriage

When it comes to men and marriage, everyone is familiar with the derisive image of a man trapped by his shrew of a wife, cuffed by his ankle to a ball and chain. He will never again taste freedom, it suggests, or have control over his own fate.

I hate that myth. But then there are nights when my husband finally returns home after traveling for several nights and I look forward to him catching up with me and taking the kids off my hands, when he turns around and tells me he's just going to change clothes so he can make it in time for a neighborhood tennis match. In those moments, for a second, I consider saying, "No! I haven't seen you in three days, and I waited to watch the next episode of *Stranger Things* on Netflix, because it's too creepy for me to watch by myself!"

But I don't. I say, "Go." And not in the "Fine, go; it's obviously what you want to do anyway, even though you have been gone for three days and I'm basically singlehandedly raising two kids" way. I seriously want him to go—because I really do care about his life outside of our home. I know he needs to have time to be competitive and social and have "who did you pick in the fantasy draft?" conversations with his buddies. I know he needs time to unwind in a way that doesn't involve picking up kids' toys off the couch and falling asleep twenty minutes into *Making a Murderer*. I get a happier, more fulfilled, more present husband and father when he gets to enjoy some time outside the home.

It took me a little bit of time to figure this out. We had many, many fights about it in our early days. I just couldn't understand why he would rather go play basketball with some sweaty guys at the gym than snuggle up with me on the couch at night. So I balked and I whined. Once we got married, I promised myself that I would *not* be the archetypal nagging wife. That I would not have the husband complaining to his buddies that he had to jet early, or else there would be hell to pay when he got home. I tried to be nice about it. Even as he would make his Saturday morning tee time with his buddies after he already played golf twice that week for work ("But honey, client golf is totally different from friend golf!"), I still tried to keep my mouth shut.

Then I started to notice results. When I didn't get jealous over his Saturday morning tee times, and didn't throw him a guilt trip or threat of retaliation—"Fine, I'll just go shopping at Louis Vuitton while you're gone!"—he would come home ready to please me. In fact, it got to the point that I didn't even mind helping him pack up his ice-water and Gatorade for his day. Because when I supported him, and was genuinely happy for him and the fun morning he was getting ready to enjoy with his buddies, he would be at my beck and call when he came home. It was like his way of saying, "Thank you. Thank you for making this easy for me, so that I don't have to coerce, plead, cajole, or worse, miss some of these parts of my life that are so important to me."

This effect kept building: the more present he was after these outings, the more supportive I became. The more supportive I became, the more he would call and check in on me, pick up my favorite lunch on the way home, and end the day a little early just to surprise me with a venti cinnamon dolce latte from Starbucks. The more I saw him think of me—worry about me while he was away—the more willing I was to give him a free pass: "Sure, go meet up with your buddies for your sixth fantasy draft pick party of the season. Totally fine!" Because I knew he would come home more ready for me, our kids, and our chaotic life.

Think of a pendulum—how it swings back and forth, but always returns to the center. Think of your marriage as the central point of the pendulum. So many things can pull you and your spouse away from each other, taking up your time, your focus, and your energy: friends, family, hobbies, birthday parties, book clubs, Bible studies, PTA meetings, soccer games, work meetings, sales goals, deadlines, conferences, seminars, volunteer work, bake sales, hair appointments, golf outings, pedicures, kickboxing classes, and wine and paint nights. And some of these things *should* pull you away. There should be space in your life and heart for things outside your home and relationship to fill you up, give you outlets, build your confidence, give you a break, provide a sense of community, and make you feel that you are not going through all this chaos alone. You should make time to do things that are fun, enjoyable, and gratifying—things that make you laugh and say, "Now, *this* is the life!" But you always want to feel the pull of the pendulum, the pull of your spouse, guiding you back to the center. And if your spouse does not feel that same pull from you, you will likely have a distressed spouse.

Troubleshooting the Unsupportive Spouse

If Julie is complaining, criticizing, or even hating the time that Bill spends away from her and doing other things, it may be because she doesn't feel that the natural pull of the pendulum is drawing him back to her—back home. She doesn't feel that when Bill is away, part of him is waiting to return to her, wanting to be with her—maybe not in that moment when he is watching the end of a tiebreaker football game with his college friends, but when the game is over and his team won and he is excited to share his experience with his spouse, to call her and say, "Did you see that last-second play? How was your time with the kids?" She may not feel the tug Bill feels toward her, toward home, when he is staying late to close that last deal at work; but she knows it's there when he calls while on his way home to say, "I did it! Let's dream together about what we're going to do with this extra money—maybe a little weekend getaway for just the two of us, since we've both been working so hard lately?" And he may not sense the tug she feels toward him during her girls' nights at the movies, when the kids aren't crawling all over her and asking for one more snack, and she's hoping the movie is a long one, so she can enjoy the peace and quiet for just a bit longer. But he feels it when she finally does get home, when she eagerly recaps the movie's surprise ending as she hands him the rest of her Sour Patch Kids—the red ones, which she saved for him, knowing they are his favorite.

Your spouse can *feel* when they are on your mind and in your heart. When your spouse can feel that you are with them, thinking of them, even when you aren't there, they do not have to hold on so tightly. They can loosen up and let go a bit, because they don't fear you won't come back. They don't fear that you don't want to come back. They don't feel you would rather be somewhere else, anywhere other than with them. Because the pull of the pendulum is strong. When they feel the strength of your desire to be with them, an amazing thing happens: instead of griping, they start supporting.

I hear this a lot in my sessions:

> *Husband: She never supports me. I don't even tell her about what's going on at work anymore, because she doesn't even care. She doesn't want to hear about it anyway. She only checks in with me during the day to see if I'm going to be late, not because she cares how my day is.*

> *Wife: Well, that's because you are always at work. It would be exhausting to check in with you all the time.*

> *Husband: The other day, I went out for happy hour with some coworkers, and she didn't ask me one question about it when I got home.*

Wife: I didn't have time to ask; I was too busy putting the kids to bed and cleaning up the kitchen—by myself.

Husband: I don't get it. I mean, am I never supposed to do anything for myself? I hardly ever play golf anymore, because I'm sick of hearing you complain about it!

Wife: Do you know how many things I've given up? Join the club!

Husband: Is that what you want? You don't want me to do anything outside of you and the kids?

Wife: I don't know anymore. Just do whatever you want. You might as well; it's what you want anyway. I surely don't want to hold you back from all the fun you are having elsewhere.

Consider another hypothetical couple, Joan and John. If Joan feels like John's life outside the home comes at her expense, she's going to be upset about it. If John comes home exhausted, depleted, with nothing left to give, she's going to start resenting the things that are happening outside the home—the things that are taking John away from her, that are getting all his time, joy, and energy. The things that are getting the best part of him, while she is left with the scraps. If she sees John's face light up when he's heading out to meet a friend for drinks, but only sees it exhausted and depleted anytime he walks through the door to greet her, she's going to feel resentful. And if she feels completely disconnected from his life outside of her, she will feel threatened by that life.

Joan can feel the disconnect if she rarely hears from John

when he is away, without a quick call, text, or even a quick pic to show her something cool he is doing. She can feel the disconnect if she can't reach him while he's gone, or if she can't feel his eagerness to include her, even if it's just to recap the conversations on the golf course that day (which, by the way, usually consist of absolutely nothing. . . . I mean, how in the heck can a group of guys spend six-plus hours together and talk about nothing of substance?). If she cannot feel John include her on some level, a competition will brew between their life at home and his life "out there"—a competition she will feel like she is losing. And she's probably going to be a sore loser.

Such a competition almost always results in a never-ending fight, because she wants him to want to be with her—even when being with her means a life full of dirty diapers, temper tantrums, homework battles, kids fighting over Pokémon cards, and falling asleep on the couch after a boring night of HGTV.

℘

My favorite movie line ever comes from The Break-Up, when Jennifer Aniston's character says, "I just want you to want to do the dishes!" Vince Vaughn's character replies, "Why in the world would anyone want to do the dishes?!" Actually, it doesn't even matter if he does the dishes. It's not about the dishes. She just wants to know that she is on his mind, that he worries about her, that he knows she is overwhelmed, and thinks, Maybe if I do the dishes for her, she won't feel so alone in this.

When your spouse spends time away from home, you should not feel that a competition exists between your spouse's outside interests and you. Instead, try to acknowledge that time for what it is: a pick-me-up for your spouse. Imagine a race car pulling into a pit stop. It gets new tires, gas, window-washing, and probably a lot of other things I'm totally unaware of, because frankly, I hate NASCAR. But the point of the stop is that it helps the car perform better. The time he spends on leisure activities outside the home—be they work outings, fantasy football drafts, golf tournaments, or tennis matches—is your husband's "pit stop." Take a moment to notice the positive impact this has on your husband. After he takes some time for himself, I bet you'll find him refreshed, grateful, appreciative, less irritable, more energetic, more excited to help out—and best of all, eager to give you the same gift in return: the gift of time away from all the chaos for a girls' weekend, bunco night, or wine-tasting party. And when you receive that gift, you have to remember this, too: he also understands you want to get away from it all from time to time, but he also needs to feel thought about, worried about and loved. He wants to feel that you may actually even *miss* home, despite the chaos. He needs to sense that you feel the pull of the pendulum too, back in his direction—and when he does, you might just be amazed at the support you get.

How to Make Your Spouse Want to Come Home to the Chaos

To strengthen the pull on the pendulum and truly reel your spouse back in after those fun outings, there needs to be some good stuff to come home to. You can make sure that happens in two ways.

First, make the time, even if it's just a brief moment within the chaos, to greet your wife or husband. Even if dinner is burning, and the kids are screaming, and the dog is barking in a scene that would make women everywhere ensure they took their birth control pill that night—give him or her a quick kiss and say, "I'm glad you're home," or have your son show off what he made at school that day. Consider that your spouse may have been yelled at by his boss or angry clients all day, and that seeing a smile on your face might be all he needs for the world to be okay again. Maybe your wife is going to be late again, and is driving home riddled with guilt over missing her daughter's soccer practice. Maybe she needs a quick hug or a hand-drawn picture from her three-year-old to let her know she is still a good mom. Sometimes, even if my kitchen looks like a bomb went off in it, I take a minute to clear the doorway of shoes and baby dolls before my husband gets home, so he doesn't trip on his way in— so he can have a moment of welcome before the house returns to chaos. These actions only take two seconds, but they can have far-reaching effects.

Second, I encourage couples to "find their jam." I'm not talking Grandma's blackberry preserves. I'm talking about finding an experience you can both enjoy together, as a couple. Sometimes you are sacrificing for your spouse—for example, when you agree to spend that coveted time away from your kids watching the 387th new *Star Wars* movie. Sometimes, he is sacrificing for you, such as when he agrees to have dinner with your new friend and her not-so-chatty, feels-like-pulling-teeth-to-get-him-to-talk husband.

But then there is that time that neither of you is sacrificing. The sweet spot, when you are both happy. Maybe you take a day trip to see your favorite country music band in concert—the band whose entire collection of albums the both of you owned, before you had ever even met. *That* is your jam. Find it, and do it often.

My husband and I both have our moments when we are sacrificing for the other. For example, my husband loves football—whereas I might care more about marching ants. In fact, I have absolutely perfected the art of staring at a football game for hours at a time, and having not one—not even *one*—thought about what is happening on that TV screen.

Chad: Did you see that crazy play?

Me: What play?

Chad: What are you doing, if you aren't watching?

Me: I have no idea.

I really wish someone would hook me up to one of those EEG machines and monitor my brain activity during a football game—I'm fairly certain the doctors would think I had slipped into a coma. I'm pretty sure I process more information in my sleep. But for my husband, waking up on a Saturday morning, looking at the lineup, making sure his Red Zone channel is working to his liking, and bantering with his friends on WhatsApp about which football team they like today is probably as close to an adult version of Christmas morning as it gets.

I have slowly but surely started to respect this reality. So what do I do? I find something that I can enjoy doing while sitting with him. He loves for me just to sit by his side. I wrote a solid 65 percent of this book while sitting next to my husband as he watched football. It was the perfect spot.

What's *my* jam? For me, it's sitting with my girlfriends on a porch filled with rocking chairs, drinking coffee and talking about nothing and everything at the same time. Whenever these opportunities arise, my husband finagles his schedule, moving around his work meetings and tennis matches so that he can stay home with the kids, and I don't have to miss these moments. It's a no-brainer in my family—not usually a conversation on *if*, but a conversation on *how*—how we can work things out so that I can be away for an afternoon, a night, a weekend.

As a marriage counselor, I sometimes experience moments when I know the sullen, panicky couple sitting in front of me is going to be fine. They are going to make it. The path to the finish line might get a little bumpy and look a little dicey, but they are going to come out ahead. I sometimes have one of these moments when I see that two partners have found their jam, when neither is sacrificing too much of himself or herself for the other.

I once counseled a couple who always seemed on the brink of divorce. Their day-to-day lives drove them to so much bickering and waffling that they threatened to separate every other day—*except* when they went to the beach. There was something about sitting by the ocean with their feet in the sand and walking hand in hand that made everything else seem petty. I found myself telling them to skip sessions and instead head to the nearest ocean. For them, visiting the beach was just as therapeutic as a counseling session.

I had another couple who wanted to pull their hair out at home. They fought constantly over who was doing more, and who was not pulling their weight. However, when they got out in the middle of nature with nothing more than a backpack and some trail mix, they felt like they had everything they needed.

I find it amazing what couples can survive. They can weather the storms of chaos. And it helps if they have their *thing*, their moment, their spot where they can reconnect.

For some couples, their *thing* is sitting together on the back patio at the day's end, listening to the crickets chirp and watching the lightning bugs through the trees. For other couples, it's the feeling they get at church, as they listen to the music and the encouraging words of their pastor. When she slips her hand in his, even though that week was *awful* and they fought like cats and dogs, everything seems better in that moment. Still others find their jam in kicking back on a blanket in the cheap seats at a baseball game, eating a hotdog, and drinking warm beer out of a Solo cup. If this one applies to you and your partner, get season tickets! Nurture these moments in your relationship, and nurture them often. To a couple wanting to connect, they are precious gifts.

You may be thinking, *My spouse and I don't have a sweet spot. What is our jam? Are we doomed?* If you *never* had a sweet spot, a moment that felt right between yourselves, you probably would never have considered saying those vows. There was *something*, somewhere, at some point, although that thing may have changed through the years. Talk about it. Work together to find it. And once you have found it, respect it.

Sitting on a porch while sipping coffee and talking for hours would be the death of my husband. I respect that. On our honeymoon, while I just wanted to bask in the sun, drift in and out of sleep, and sip mai tais, my husband was poking me in the arm every five minutes, saying, "Wanna go snorkel? Wanna throw a football on the beach? Wanna take a swim? Take a hike? Take a drive?" I responded: "*Nooo!* I just want to sit here and do nothing!"

Sitting on the beach together—not our jam. Renting a Jeep the next day, packing up a lunch, exploring waterfalls, jumping over the sign that said "BEWARE!" and finding the coolest spot that overlooked peaks and valleys in the middle of nowhere? That was our jam. Taking a trip to Europe and exploring castles, art museums, and ancient ruins? Not our jam. While I listened to the audio tour at Westminster Abbey, he was sitting on a pew, bored and looking up local pubs on his iPhone. But taking a train to a tiny Swiss town and checking into a quaint hotel, skiing till our muscles ached and our legs gave out, hiding our heads in shame as we took the gondola back down the mountain because we couldn't manage to ski the last run on our weary legs, jumping in a taxi to go back to the hotel, and soaking in the hot tub? That was our jam.

Find yours. Look at pictures; talk to other couples to get suggestions; look through travel magazines and websites. Look up weekend events in your local newspaper. Look for volunteer work to do together. Find a cause you both believe in, some activity that lets you both feel satisfaction in your hearts, and do it together. Look for something that makes you both say, "That could be fun!" or "That could be meaningful to us." Then do it, and if it is fun or meaningful, do it a lot. Congratulations—you have found your jam.

You Always Have
a Part in the Problem

Always, always, always. You *always* have a part in the problem. Not just a little bit; not just in certain circumstances. Always.

Some of you are probably reading this right now, thinking, *But if you only knew what happened to me! If you only knew what my spouse has done—how I was so terribly wronged, even though I was doing everything I was supposed to be doing! I was doing everything right, and then this all happened to me!* To you, I would still say, "Always. You *always* have a part in the problem!"

It was actually quite the relief to learn this as a marriage counselor. When I first started out, I used to listen to both sides, with my teeth chattering and my mind spinning because *he made a good point, but so did she!* And I could totally see her side of things—*but wait, I didn't think about that. Yes, that sounds right, too! Ugh! Who is right in this?* I knew I needed to call for reinforcements. I decided to explain it all to my supervisor, and await the final verdict. Who would it be? The spineless husband who sided with his mom instead of his wife, or the manipulative wife who knowingly left her mother-in-law off the birthday party guest list? I could hardly wait. It was more exciting than an episode of *Law and Order: SVU*—and I love Olivia Benson and Elliott Stabler.

I anxiously sat and waited as my supervisor mulled it over. Who was it, already? The suspense was killing me!

After careful consideration, my supervisor said, "It seems like you are getting caught up in the content of their fight. You need to help them learn to see how they got to that point, how they both contribute to the problem, how they're in an endless cycle that can be seen in countless other situations in their marriage."

Wait, what? You aren't going to *tell* me? You aren't going to end this once and for all? How can I possibly help them and tell them what to do if I don't know who is to blame? Does he need to quit drinking, or does she need to loosen up? Was she talking to that man in a flirty way, or is he just being insecure? Is he a messy slob, or does she have OCD? Is he a lazy bum who doesn't help with the kids, or is she a super-controlling know-it-all who insists on doing it all herself? I was planning to sit back in my expert chair, hear both arguments, bang my gavel, and say, "You are the one! You are guilty! Guilty as charged!" How can I do that, when both parties are at fault?

Is It Your Fault or Mine?

So here it is—the answer to the problems in your marriage. The reason I get paid the big bucks. The answer to all your troubles, all your woes, all your strife. Drumroll, please . . .

It's because you did *this,* and then he did *that,* and then you did *this* and he did *that.* And this went on for days, months, and years.

Now that we have that figured out, what to do? I want you to spend some time in deep reflection—in real consideration—recognizing that you did some things wrong, which in turn encouraged *him* to do some things wrong, which in turn encouraged *you* to do some things wrong. If you are willing to dare, willing to open yourself up to this possibility, the idea that maybe you—yes, you—were part of this, too, then there is hope for your relationship yet.

Now, there are certain situations, such as an affair, that can tempt spouses to ignore the idea that "two people contributed to the problem." If your spouse has had an affair, I'm not suggesting you consider how you may have contributed to that particular affair per se, but rather how you may have contributed to the divide in the relationship that created a window for the affair to happen. When did the divide occur? Where did the crack start? And how did that crack get so wide that it allowed someone else to get in? I want to assure you that in no way was your spouse's affair your fault. Read that sentence again. It might help you digest these words: it was not your fault your spouse chose to have an affair. No one had a gun to their head. They had a million other choices in how they could have handled the disconnect they experienced in the relationship. Furthermore, the affair didn't happen because you weren't attractive enough, skinny enough, muscular enough, perfect enough, clean enough, successful enough, rich enough, smart enough, young enough, or funny enough. But somehow, a crack opened in your relationship. I'm encouraging you to consider how you *both* contributed to the formation of that crack.

Don't do it on day one. If you are just learning of an affair and still reeling from the shock of it, take some time. Grieve, cry, scream, yell, hurt. Do all that for as long as you need; but if you are considering repairing the relationship at some point, take a look at how this happened. It's reasonable to be curious, and it will help you make sense of things. It will help your anger fade; it will help you recover; and it will help to ensure that you never get back to that spot again.

I remember a couple, Lauren and Jeff, who came to me after Lauren learned of Jeff's emotional affair with a coworker. I learned that Lauren doted over Jeff and was consumed by thoughts of how to make him happy. She prioritized the relationship over everything else—which was as she thought all good marriages should be. She obsessed over whether Jeff was having a good or bad day, which was especially difficult for her as Jeff was very quiet, reserved, and stoic. She often couldn't tell what was on his mind or how he was feeling. She pressed harder and harder to find out. Sometimes she got accusatory, demanding, and at times, demeaning. He became more and more stoic.

As they talked about the affair and how it had happened, Jeff opened up about how suffocated, trapped, and overwhelmed he felt by her constant pressure, her constant focus on him. He was so consumed each day with trying to talk her off a ledge that he felt he couldn't tell her how overwhelmed and desperate he was starting to feel for peace, or for a bit more independence. He didn't want to give her more ammunition for her obsession.

After Lauren interrupted Jeff for the third time during our session to tell him how wrong he was in how he saw things, he got frustrated. He said, "This is why I don't share things with you—because you tell me I'm wrong, and that what I think and feel is wrong. I don't even bother talking to you anymore."

It was at that moment that Lauren stopped. After a few minutes of silence, she quietly and humbly said, "Is that why you reached out to her instead of me?"

He tearfully nodded and said, "Yes. And I know it was wrong. And as soon as I started to notice I was having feelings for her, I stopped all contact. But it was just so nice to have someone to listen to me and understand. I felt sad that she seemed to understand me while you didn't."

Lauren responded in the most genuine manner, and I can still remember the power of her words. She said, "I'm still so hurt, so betrayed by you; but I also want to know how to do this differently—how to respond to you in ways that let you know I understand you. I want to understand you. I think I need help in learning how. I would like to try to do it differently."

I could have stood up and hugged her in that moment, I was so proud of her.

In marriage, a state of disconnection can be a breeding ground for betrayals such as an affair. In order to work toward healing a relationship that has been shaken by an affair, we have to figure out when and where the disconnect started. And I truly believe there is nothing harder than feeling betrayed on such a deep level and still being able to step back and look at your own part of the disconnect. It takes incredible bravery for people to look at their part in a situation that has brought them so much pain.

I have a friend whom I call when I get really worked up about my husband. I call her specifically because she is not going to let me off the hook. She is not going to buy my BS about how *he did this, and this, and that!* while I did nothing but stand there, talk sweetly, and look pretty. No, I didn't. I did *something*. It may not be obvious, and it may not be flattering, but I did it. And often, I need help seeing it.

Find someone who can help you to see your side, too—a neutral bystander, a loving friend, someone who will hold your feet to the fire. If you are always choosing to confide in the superfriend extraordinaire who will always take your side and support you no matter what, you are in bad hands. You need someone to help you see how you pulled away—how you got too busy with work or too involved with the kids; were cruel in your words, antagonistic, shortsighted, and dismissive; didn't listen; stopped asking for what you needed because you didn't want to be a burden; started to get bitter and angry and spiteful because you weren't getting what you wanted; started to shut down and turn away because you were hurt; and started neglecting your marriage. And in turn, your spouse did a whole bunch of things wrong, too.

How did those things go wrong? Sometimes it's hard to figure that out. You do know that your relationship didn't always feel this way; you used to feel loved, supported, cared for, appreciated, respected, and connected. You don't know what happened. When a couple first comes to me, neither do I. But after some reflection, some guidance, and some good counsel, we can start to see. We can start to see how you did *this*, and then he did *that*, and then she did *that*, and you did *this*. Then and only then can we do anything about it.

My husband has a few hang-ups. One of these is the sound of food being chewed. He hates it. If I'm eating a late-night snack of popcorn, I need to sit on the other side of the couch with the volume on the TV up about seven notches so that I don't bother him. It also turns out he hates how loudly I breathe when I sleep. And most recently, I learned that I apparently walk around the house with a heavy tread that wakes him up early in the morning. So sorry, dear. So sorry I eat and breathe and walk around my own home, which I help pay for. Did you ever think that maybe you have a superhuman sense of hearing? Did you ever think that maybe this is your fault, too?! It is. I have tried to be a bit more mindful of chewing crunchy things in his earshot. I've softened my steps on the stairs in the early morning, and I sleep a bit more to the left, so that he can't hear my "loud" breathing. But he also knows that his hang-ups may be just a bit over-the-top, and that I don't need to change a thing. And he knows that he loves me anyway—loud breathing, heavy walking, loud chewing and all.

Learn Your Old Path, Find a New Path

I talk a lot in therapy about old paths and new paths—the ways we're used to dealing with conflict and emotions, and the new and better ways we *want* to deal with those things. When it comes to the way we deal with our spouse, we can't change the old path if we don't know what it is. And the old path is *never* "I sat here perfectly while *you* screwed it up." More likely, the old path looks like this:

> *Wife: Seriously?! You are so busy looking at your precious phone that you knocked over my glass! I'm not asking for much here. I already made dinner, washed the kids' hands, and got their lunches ready for tomorrow. If you aren't going to help, at least stay out of my way!*
>
> *Husband: Fine, I will! Since I obviously make things worse, I'll just stay out of your way altogether!*
>
> *Wife: I'm sure that's what you want anyway—now you can take all the time you need with your phone and computer and iPad and everything else you would rather be doing!*

Husband (walking away and muttering under his breath): I can't even knock over a glass without you freaking out. You obviously have major issues.

Wife: That's right! Just walk away like you always do. I can't bring up anything without you running away. Everything is off-limits. I don't even know why I bother.

In order to get on a new path, we have to understand the old path. We have to understand why he did the things he did, and why she did the things she did—because if we don't, in the heat of the moment, that old path can emerge and reestablish itself in ten seconds or less. We have to understand that he shut down and walked away because he felt attacked and inadequate when she fussed at him. We have to understand that she fussed at him because she felt unimportant and ignored. We have to understand that when he walked away, she thought, *He only cares about himself, and obviously doesn't care that I am hurting.* And we have to understand that when he walked away, it wasn't because he didn't care. It was because he felt angry and hurt and was scared that if he stayed, he would say something that would make things worse, so his only recourse was to lock himself in his office in the hope that the moment would pass, she would cool down, and things would be good again.

When we examine the old path, we begin to understand that in moments like those, he gets scared that one more screw-up may be the final straw that makes her see she doesn't want him anymore. He wants to give her what she wants, but he doesn't feel that he knows how. So he sits and waits and hopes that things will improve with time.

And we have to understand that while he sits and waits, she feels that he doesn't care about her. She is hurt and angry at that thought, especially after everything she has poured into their family today, yesterday, this week, this year. We have to understand that while he sits behind that office door, she starts to think, *He doesn't even want a partner*, or *He's just not capable of giving me what I need.* And sometimes she thinks, *Maybe he just doesn't even want me. He's more interested in his job, his computer, his iPhone than me.* We have to understand that what she needs more than anything in that moment is to hear that he cares about her; that she is important to him, more important than everything else, and he wants to be there for her, even if he feels like he doesn't know how.

We have to understand that when he finally emerges from that office and sees her hurt, angry glare, he withdraws even further and misses his chance, because he feels like he is the last person in the world she wants to see right then. Even though she so desperately wants him to hug her and tell her he is there for her, her resentful expression sends him silently screaming in the other direction. It seems impossible for him to make it right. So he's too scared to try, too scared to reach out to comfort her.

We have to understand that when he feels like he has really blown it, like he has let her down—like, no matter what, he cannot make her happy—he needs to know that she loves him. That even though she is angry and disappointed, it is because she cares so much about him that his actions hurt—because she loves him and he matters to her.

We have to understand these things. And when we do, we can construct a new path, one that looks more like this:

> *Wife: Seriously?! You are so busy looking at your precious phone that you knocked over my glass! I'm not*

asking for much here. I already made dinner, washed the kids' hands, got their lunches ready for tomorrow. If you aren't going to help, at least stay out of my way!

Wait—I'm sorry I snapped. It's just that sometimes I feel like you care more about your phone than you do about me. I know you have a lot going on and it's hard to tear yourself away from work sometimes, but I look forward to this time at the end of the day when we can actually have a few minutes together. I really value this time with you. And sometimes, when you seem distracted and focused on your phone and work, I start to question whether you value this time with me. I'm trying not to get angry when I feel like I'm not a priority, and instead just let you know when it feels that way. I just need to know I'm more important than your work.

Husband: I know, I know. I get so distracted at times. I'm trying to get better at putting my work down and putting my phone away so I can be with you and the kids. I'm still struggling with that, but I appreciate you apologizing for snapping and letting me know. I do value this time with you, too, and I'm hoping I can show you that better. I know sometimes I don't act like you are a priority, but you are. Really, the biggest reason I focus so much on work and get so distracted is because I want to provide for us, because you and the kids are so important to me. I kind of feel like it's my main job, and sometimes I let that consume me.

Wife: I know you work hard. I know you want to be a good provider, and you are. But more important than all that is just to be together and put it all aside, even for five minutes. We kinda like having you here, you know?

Husband: I do. And I like being here, too. I'm sorry I don't always make that very easy to see. But it helps to know that you want me around. I'm going to put my phone in the office during dinner. It'll be just me at dinnertime from now on. It would also help me if you tried to understand how hard it is for me to achieve that balance at times. I am going to try harder to be focused, but I also need to know that you appreciate me and how hard I work to support us.

What many couples fail to see is that there is often an amazing love story under their struggles. Often he did *this* and she did *that* because they care so much about each other and are so sensitive to what the other thinks, acts, and feels. The sensation of spinning around in a conflict that can feel never-ending is due to the emotions, reactions, and turmoil that ensues when a relationship feels threatened or disconnected, because these two people are so important to each other, so sensitive to each other—because they *do* care, so much.

Couples often forget that they want the same thing from each other: to be needed, desired, cherished, supported, appreciated, loved, and cared for. They want these things not from any Jack or Jill on the street, but from their spouse, the person they married, the one with whom they decided to go through this whole thing called life. Often, this mutual desire is so hidden beneath a big pile of back-and-forth that couples have difficulty seeing that it exists. They even start to convince themselves that it doesn't.

Why Can't I See My Part? Why Can't My Spouse See Theirs?

If you are having trouble seeing your part in the conflict you are having with your spouse, please consider: marital conflict always takes two people.

In your or your spouse's defense, some people have never been taught to take responsibility for their part in a conflict, because they weren't taught that you can screw up, get it wrong, make a huge mess of things, and *still* be loved, cared for, wanted, and accepted. If this was never part of your experience growing up—if you never saw your parents humble themselves and say to you, "I was wrong. I shouldn't have yelled at you like that—I'm sorry," if you never heard them say, "Yes, you screwed up, but we love you just the same—there is nothing you could do to change that"—if your parents never listened to your side, or considered your heart or your intentions without doling out severe punishment—then admitting to any fault during a conflict can feel like foreign territory. You may never have experienced the freedom in being able to see your part. You may have had so much practice defending yourself in an effort to receive approval, appreciation, support, love, and care that you always feel you are in a fight for your life when someone is upset with you. When things aren't going well, you get into an argument that could impress even the shrewdest defense attorney.

But now, it's time to take a look, and see your part in your marital conflict. Because here's the thing: when you don't consider your part, you become more frustrated, upset, and angry that you are *still* not getting what you want from your spouse. And when you feel that all the responsibility lies with your partner, you are left in what feels like a hopeless, powerless position, as you wait for him or her to change.

If you are unsure whether you are one of those people who have a difficult time seeing their part in a conflict, consider these red flags:

Red Flags That Show You Can't See Your Part in a Conflict

- You complain about your spouse all the time.
- You confide in those who will complain with you. ("Oh, your husband did that? Listen to what *my* husband did!")
- You keep a mental laundry list of all the ways he or she has wronged you.
- You keep score.
- You say things like, "I'm know I'm not perfect either," but you have no other description for your behavior.
- Your spouse often says things like, "Oh, right, since you are just so perfect!" in a sarcastic tone.
- You can't remember the last time you said, "I'm sorry."
- You are reading this chapter and thinking, *I'm sure this applies to lots of people, but it doesn't apply to me.* (It does.)
- You are thinking, *This applies to me in some of our conflicts, but not in others.* (It *always* applies.)
- You are reading this right now, and highlighting every part so that you can show it to your spouse later, because they *never* think they are to blame, and they *always* blame you.

The Way Out

Now you need a way out. You need to see how when he did *that,* you did *this,* and then he did *that,* which kept you from what you both wanted: to feel loved, appreciated, supported, connected, calmed, cared for, and prioritized. There are some very skilled people out there who can help you see how you are getting in your own way—how when you change how you respond like *this,* then he changes how he reacts like *that.* It's quite amazing.

Think about a game of table tennis. Think about how just a slight twist of your wrist makes the ball go in a completely different direction, which makes your opponent leap to the other side of the table to hit it back. It turns out you have a lot of power, but it helps to know that sometimes, despite your best intentions, despite your best efforts, and in spite of the fact that you have care in your heart, you get in your own way. Sometimes you just need someone to look in and say, "Oh, all your troubles are happening because you do *this* and then she does *that!* That's why! How about instead, you do *that,* and I bet she will do *this.*"

I know I'm making this sound easy—as if I'm implying all your years of frustrations and sufferings can be fixed easily, with the flick of your wrist. I assure you that's not the case. Do you know why? Because you have been reacting to certain triggers in a certain way for a really long time, even before you realized you were doing so, before it had a significant impact on someone you love. And because you have very valid reasons for having those reactions.

I grew up in the country, where for eighteen years, I had to drive down the same long country highway and take a right on Whipple Trail to get to my parents' house, right past the general store. Then my parents moved about a mile farther down the street, so instead of turning on Whipple Trail, I had to start taking a left onto Golden Drive. This was almost like a cruel joke. My entire life, I had automatically, thoughtlessly turned right on Whipple Trail. Now, I had to take my brain off autopilot. I had to pay attention, look at my surroundings, and focus, so that I wouldn't do what my brain and body had done so many times before. But it wasn't easy. It was like my car had a magnet on it that was always pulled to that 1976 yellow split-level house on Whipple Trail. I had to ignore that magnet and put in an amount of brainpower and effort I never had to before, just to get home.

The truth is, I ended up in the driveway in front of my old home more times than I will ever admit. I even got out a few times and walked up the driveway, wondering why my parents had children's toys in their front yard.

Change is hard.

One could look at my struggle and say, "Oh, you should just move back to your old street, and then you wouldn't have to worry about going the wrong way all the time!" No! The answer was to slow down, turn down the radio so I could pay attention, look for landmarks, get my bearings—and, when I still went down my old street, to stop, take a deep breath, and turn around and try again tomorrow.

The answer isn't necessarily a new house or a new partner. Sometimes it's a new technique, a new way of responding, a new approach. And then, lo and behold, that becomes your new normal.

I still drive by my old street when I visit my parents, and instead of accidentally turning right and exclaiming, "Crap! I'm such an idiot! They don't live here anymore!" I speed by and say, "Brooklyn, look! It's Mommy's old street! That's where Mommy grew up!"

That street is a distant memory now. I drive a new path, and you can, too. It's a much easier fight to change a way of expressing, responding, recognizing, and connecting than it is to change an entire person or personality.

Let's talk about the do-it-yourself remedy—because as much

as I would love for someone to help you get your marriage out of this nasty cycle, some people just aren't up for it. They aren't up for exposing their insides to a complete stranger. Weird, huh? I mean, why *wouldn't* you want to saunter into a therapist's office, sit down with someone you've never met and know absolutely nothing about, and say, "Here it is, the stuff I've told no one, the stuff I haven't even told my own spouse; here it is for you, stranger! Here it is for you to see and judge, critique, and tell me what I'm doing wrong." I can't imagine why someone wouldn't want to do that! And let's face it: Google can tell us pretty much everything we need to know these days anyway, right? I'll take my kids to the doctor if they are so much as looking at me funny, but me? I basically need to be having a life-or-death crisis before I will see a doctor. Otherwise, I just pop open my WebMD app, check the boxes that apply to me, and await my diagnosis. So I get it.

Here are a few DIY tips. First, there is no better way to start seeing your part than by staying curious. Curiosity is the complete opposite of defensiveness. Allow me to illustrate this point.

Amanda came to couples counseling with her husband, Jacob. She described how Jacob would shut down and avoid opening up to her. She described how, anytime she brought up anything important, he got silent—or worse, walked away without saying a word. She described feeling so frustrated that she could never bring up anything of importance without him withdrawing.

As Jacob sat quietly, she looked at me and said, "Do you see what I deal with? He's impossible. I can't be in a relationship with someone who won't talk to me!"

I get it. It's painful to be shut out from the one person in the world whom you want to know and feel close to, feel connected to. But this is when you have to channel your inner curiosity—your inner Nancy Drew or Perry Mason (or maybe someone a little more modern and trendier). Then, instead of "You never open up to me," you can say, "Is there something I'm doing or not doing that is keeping you from feeling safe enough to open up to me and tell me what is going on for you? Because I'm really sad that you don't open up to me, and I'm really curious how I might be shutting you down or pushing you away from me. I feel like maybe I'm not seeing it, so I'm open to your feedback. It would be helpful if you could be gentle in giving me this feedback, so that I can stay open and not become defensive."

Second, try to get input from someone you trust—someone to whom you can say, "Hey, you see me interact with my spouse and hear my stories about our struggles. Is there something that I may not be seeing? Is there something you see me doing that is making this worse?"

A good friend of mine once went to a therapist who asked her to write a few questions to send to her closest friends and gather their responses. The questions were, "What do you see as my strengths and weaknesses in relationships?" and "What do you hope I learn to do different in my relationships?"

I loved this. I loved that my friend was so eager, open, and willing to ask questions that left her vulnerable, in an effort to do things differently.

Be eager. Be curious. Ask questions. You may be amazed at what you learn. And you may have more influence than you think.

I remember one of my favorite "ah-ha" moments from my work with a couple named Kelly and Jason. They came for therapy after a short but traumatic separation. Jason had packed his bags and left, leaving Kelly feeling utterly devastated—the kind of devastation that made it hard for her even to catch her breath as she described to me what had happened.

They explained that they had gotten back together and decided they wanted to make things work, to make things right between them. Jason knew he had traumatized her and broken her trust when he had stormed out. As we talked about how things had gotten to that point—how, on that specific day, he'd felt he couldn't do it anymore—I learned that Kelly had said some hurtful words to him, the type of words she had heard a million times in her household while she was growing up. They didn't seem like a big deal to her.

Jason described how her words had hit him like a ton of bricks. To him, those words had made it seem that she thought he was the absolute scum of the earth.

After he emotionally described the extent to which her words impacted him, Kelly kept saying something I will never forget. Over and over, she said, "I just can't believe it. I just can't believe it." She continued, "I mean, I believe him; I believe what he is saying, that my actions affected him that deeply. I just can't believe I have that type of impact on him. I would have never guessed in a million years that I could affect him like that."

I always love these moments, when a partner truly gets it. I love it when they understand how much they impact their partner, for better or for worse. For the first time, Kelly learned how important she was to Jason, and how much he cared about how she saw him. She learned the power of her words and actions. Although she still couldn't believe that she was truly so important to him, she did believe him. She was finally able to see her part in the problem.

That day, due to her openness, Kelly received a gift of power. She now had the power to choose how she wanted to impact her spouse. And because she wanted to impact him in positive ways, she became careful with her words. She even started to feel confident that he would never leave her again, because she knew she could ensure that she never made him feel that way again. And then, for the first time since he had left her and returned, she felt she could breathe.

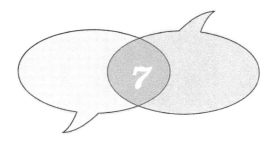

There Is No Room for Secrecy

Marriage counselors can often sense when a member of a couple is keeping secrets. They can feel it in their bones. Something feels off. Something isn't lining up. Something is missing. And usually, they are right. There is something that is not being said, and often, it's the elephant in the room.

Call them what you want—omissions, lies, withholdings, things you didn't say and hoped would never be found out. Things that made you tell yourself, "It's no big deal; everyone has their secrets. We don't have to tell each other everything!" You are right: you don't have to tell him about what you ate for lunch; you don't have to tell her about your weird bathroom habits. Some aspects of life can and should be reserved for your eyes and ears only. But you know the difference between "I don't want him to know I ate the entire bag of pretzel M&Ms in one sitting, so I hid the empty bag in the bottom of the trash," and "I hope she doesn't check the credit card statement and see that I withdrew $200 to bet on that game, even though I promised her I was done betting." It is the difference between privacy and secrecy. And there is no room for secrecy in a marriage.

I remember when I first learned this heart-stopping fact.

When I first started as a therapist, I had the amazing opportunity to complete my internship at a renowned practice in Scottsdale, Arizona, called Psychological Counseling Services. I got to sit in with skilled and seasoned therapists who helped couples heal from severe betrayals, and often countless infidelities. Clients were encouraged to "lay it all out there," to share the extent of what had been done, to their sometimes unsuspecting spouse.

I remember thinking, *Do we really have to tell him? Can't we just let him stay in la-la land for a bit longer? I mean, this is going to change everything! This is going to wreck his world!* My supervisor would say, "There is no room for secrets in a marriage." I remember thinking, *Are you sure? What about little ones, ones that happened so long ago that no one really cares about them now? What about the ones that would only hurt him, or her—isn't it better to spare their feelings? Isn't it just better to keep those to yourself? Surely you just mean* some *secrets, or* certain *secrets, or maybe just the really bad ones. You can't really mean* all *secrets! That sounds crazy!*

Isn't It Better to Keep the Peace?

I grew up in a family that didn't talk about difficult things. We kept conversations simple, easy—safe. As far as I knew, the biggest problems my parents had were agreeing on who had left the refrigerator door open and deciding how I was going to get to soccer practice. Let's just say no one ever rocked the boat.

As I listened to my supervisor reply, "Yes, you should tell her that—oh, yes, and that, too—can't keep that to yourself, either," I thought, *Wait a minute! Isn't it better to keep the peace? It's so nice! I had such a peaceful childhood, one full of rainbows and butterflies; and even if it was all a façade, isn't it so nice to be left in the dark? Not to have a worry in the world?*

Here's the problem: secrecy creates distance. It's true that as a child, I didn't need to know all the ins and outs of money troubles, family blowups, or skeletons in the family closet. It's appropriate to maintain a careful flow of information from a parent to a child. But not between spouses.

Something I went on to learn is that the wife who has just learned that her husband had an affair with their realtor—the woman who shook her hand and looked her in the eye and told her, "Congratulations on your new home! You and your family are going to be so happy here!"—may not have suspected her husband was having that specific affair, but she did suspect *something*. And it had been nagging at her for days, months—maybe years, before the truth came out. She had either turned that gut feeling into countless accusations and done everything short of putting her husband on house arrest, which in turn had led to countless blowout fights—or she had been consumed with wondering why he seemed so distant. Was it something she did, something she said? Was it because she didn't look like she used to before the kids and the twenty-plus years since they had gone on their first date, when she was twenty-five pounds lighter? Then, as she had criticized herself and assumed she must be the problem, she'd started to feel depressed, though she couldn't figure out why. Why, when she had everything she'd ever wanted in life—a nice house, beautiful children, a successful husband— why couldn't she drag herself out of bed on most days? "What is wrong with me?" she'd wondered.

Secrets can be painful, but telling them can set a person free. I remember one of my couples who were fighting bitterly. She ended up revealing that she'd had a one-night stand at a recent work conference. When he angrily left the room and threatened not to return (he did), she turned to me and said, "See, I shouldn't have told him! Now everything is ruined! I should have just kept it a secret."

I turned to her and said, "It wasn't the telling of the secret that ruined anything. It was the affair. The telling of the secret is your one shot at making it right."

There is always a fallout to keeping secrets. When they are withheld, that fallout is distance, and arguments that go around and around as couples try to figure out how to close a gap that can't be closed—not with secrets in the way. Secrets kill intimacy, and the result is always the same: distance.

Secrets also often lead to more secrets. He can't deal with the shame of secretly gambling away his savings, so he stops at the bar on the way home to have a few drinks and calls his wife to tell her he is running late at a meeting. When he gets home and sees her sullen face, he can't handle the shame of his most recent lie and blows up at her for not remembering to pick up the dry cleaning. He feels incredible remorse when he sees the scared look in her eye, so he locks himself in his office and starts to text an old girlfriend who he knows will respond in a flirty way, which will make him feel better. To hide the flirtatious text messages between them, he deletes the contents of his phone. When his wife looks at his phone later that night to get the phone number for their plumber, she sees the deleted history and asks him about it. He accuses her of being nosy and overbearing.

It is then that this pair comes into a couples session—where we spend the entire session talking about her nosiness, and how she doesn't respect his privacy. And all the while, these huge, life-altering secrets lurk in the background!

As I think of my own marriage, sifting through my mind for

examples of my husband and me working through secrets, I can't find one. We don't keep secrets. That has been a priority, a non-negotiable facet of our marriage since we said, "I do."

I once ran into an ex-boyfriend at the grocery store. We chatted briefly, and he told me about his marriage and divorce, his ailing father, his new nephew, and his new job. I came home and shared this news with my husband. As I relayed our conversation, my husband stopped me midsentence and said, "Why are you telling me all this? I don't want to hear all these things about your ex!" I said, "I'm not telling you because I think you care. I'm telling you because I want to be transparent. I want you to know the content of our conversation so that you are always in the know. I don't want you to feel like I kept something like this from you. That's why I'm telling you."

He smiled and said, "Oh, that makes sense. Okay, you can continue."

Secrecy Versus Transparency

The opposite of secrecy is transparency—the feeling that exists between two people when they are both "in the know," when they have all the information; the feeling that if they had eyes on their spouse every day, they wouldn't be surprised or upset by what they saw.

I have worked with couples who have been through all levels of infidelity, from emotional affairs to full-blown double lives that have passed under their spouse's radar for decades. One of the questions I like to ask is, "If your spouse followed you around each day, how often would they be upset by what they saw? How often would they be upset at the way your eyes lingered, your tone became flirty when an attractive coworker entered the room, or your conversation became a bit too personal?"

It's fairly obvious to each partner that their spouse would be upset if they saw them engaging in any physical, romantic, or intimate contact with another person. But subtler betrayals can often be bypassed, justified, overlooked, or minimized. In sessions, I would often hear, "He's just a friend. I just needed someone to talk to, and he's a good listener. It's not a big deal; you're just overreacting." Or, "What? I can't talk to *any* woman now—they're all off-limits? You're being so unrealistic!" Or, "She just gets so jealous. We are working on the same project, so we *have* to travel to the same places and stay in the same hotel. The company plans all that; there's nothing I can do about it. She just needs to get over it." Chances are she won't—unless he acknowledges the vulnerability of the situation and take actions to protect himself from those vulnerabilities. And the first way to do this is to understand how these subtle betrayals can happen.

Let me illustrate. Rachel and Tim work together. They are assigned to collaborate on a project. They realize they get more done without the distractions at the office, so they meet at a lunch spot on the corner. They chat about their jobs, their annoying coworkers, their demanding boss. They learn details about each other's families, like the ages of the kids, what schools they attend, and where they grew up or went to college. Seems harmless, right?

The next day, Rachel dresses a bit cuter. While he waits for her to get off the phone, Tim lingers in front of her office to see if she wants to join him again for lunch, to flesh out some details of their project. She does. They talk more. Rachel complains about how much her husband travels, and confides that she has started to wonder whether they are living more like roommates than spouses. Tim tells her that her husband sounds like an idiot; if *Tim* had a wife like Rachel, he would surely appreciate her. Tim talks about his wife and how she used to be cool and laid-back—"but since the twins were born, she has become so uptight, such a control freak." He thinks they are just becoming different people now, with different interests. Things change, you know?

Rachel does know. She fully agrees. And tomorrow they will meet again, and share more and more about their spouses who just don't listen, who don't understand—not like Rachel does, not like Tim does. "Gosh, it just feels so nice to talk to someone who listens! Someone who gets it! Isn't this so nice?"

If you are reading this and do not see the problem, or if you are reading this and it feels all too familiar, let me put a label on it. Rachel and Tim are venturing into an emotional affair. They are confiding in another, hearing the confidences of another, and their spouses are none the wiser. They are also comparing apples to oranges, weighing the complicated intimacy that develops between spouses who deal with the daily toils of long hours, poopy diapers, and hurt feelings against a new, easy, unreactive conversation with someone who is putting their best foot forward—someone who hasn't been hurt by comments, actions, and behaviors for the past twelve years. But in reality, there is no comparison. One is real life; the other is fantasy.

Ever since we got married, my husband has been my primary confidant. I still confide in my girlfriends, too; often, my husband would rather not be the one to hear about my best friend's neighbor's sister's new baby, or how I feel about the cast ABC just picked for the new season of *The Bachelorette*. But when it comes to every important matter, I confide in him.

But what sorts of matters are important, and what can be

considered frivolous? What type of information carries significant emotional weight, and what doesn't? This is where things can get tricky. A lot of couples do not know when they are crossing the line. They do not see how they are wading into dangerous territory when they are chatting it up with their personal trainer at the gym, or how late nights on work trips with their attractive colleague can tempt even the untemptable. They don't realize that when they are revealing their complaints about their marriage to their hairstylist and hear, "Gosh, she sounds like a nag—it seems like she doesn't appreciate you," they could be flirting with the start of an emotional affair. They are on the dangerous ground of confiding in another woman or man who is not their spouse, without their spouse's knowledge. At the same time, they may not realize that when they offered an empathetic listening ear to their boss—whose wife doesn't realize how much he sacrifices for the family, or how good she has it—they are standing on equally shaky ground.

I Can't Tell—My Spouse Will Freak Out!

You may have read my example about running into my ex and thought, "No way I would tell my wife if I ran into one of *my* exes! She would just freak out! It's not worth bringing it up!"

Here's the thing: she freaks out because there is some reason she doesn't trust you. Instead of calling her insecure and jealous, seek to understand. First, do you keep secrets? Are you transparent in your interactions with your spouse? If you are not, then guess what? She can feel that. She can feel the space between you, and it frightens her. That fear turns to anxiety, and that anxiety can come out in the form of an interrogation that would make Jack Bauer from *24* seem like a lightweight. If you aren't transparent, you need to accept the consequences—and the consequences typically look like a jealous, angry, overcontrolling, insecure spouse.

There is another option. Maybe you *are* truly on the up and up. You actually *wish* she would hire a private detective to follow you around, so that you can prove yourself once and for all: "I'm not doing anything! I'm trustworthy! You can trust me! What more can I do to prove that?" If this is you, then I encourage you to explore the possibility that the root of your spouse's anxiety is not you, but in something borne out of her past. Perhaps her trust in others has been broken so many times that even though she wants to trust you, history tells her that it is not safe. I sometimes hear, "I feel like if I take my eyes off the ball for one second, I'll miss it—I'll miss the one clue that shows me he is up to no good, and I'll look like a fool, like I did in my last relationship, when I was completely blindsided." So she stays vigilant, and often accusatory.

My husband and I can sometimes be terrible at communicating our daily plans. He will call and say, "Did I tell you I had to stay overnight at work tonight?" Nope, you didn't. But for me, that's no big deal. Why? Because I trust him. He has never given me any reason *not* to trust him. And, further, I have not been blindsided in the past. I haven't experienced the fallout of betrayal, so I'm not hypersensitive to it. I have many other vulnerabilities, but this is not one of them. My husband and I have a bit more flexibility in this. We can spring things on each other, and it doesn't rock the boat.

But not everyone has this luxury. Some people have been hurt; their trust has been broken, and now they are sensitive. This is nothing to throw in their faces! Quite the opposite. If your spouse is one of these people, try to be sensitive in those moments and figure out what helps, what makes him or her feel safer with you. Does it help to keep a Google family planner, so she can prepare for your absences ahead of time? Does it help if you check in during the day a bit more often, maybe with a text or phone call, just to touch base? Does it help if you call her as soon as you get to your hotel room at night, so she can hear you are there alone? Heck, maybe she even needs a FaceTime view of the room. Not forever—but maybe for a bit, until she starts to relax and feel safe.

Early on in my relationship with my husband, Chad, we started meeting each other's friends and family. Naturally, I wanted rave reviews from his friends. Once, we joined them to watch a football game. As I sat next to one of his friends, we laughed and joked about our favorite *Seinfeld* episodes. I was already visualizing the A-plus rating I was earning—one that would inevitably be shared with my new boyfriend after I left.

When the game ended, Chad and I got in the car, and he was silent. And it wasn't the typical sweet, calm, comfortable silence he fell into when he wanted to hold hands at the end of the night, but two-hands-on-the-steering-wheel, staring-straight-ahead silence. I had no idea what had happened. What did I miss? What did I do?

It turned out he felt that I was acting very flirty with his friend. In fact, one of his other friends had actually made a comment about my flirtatious tone, and noticed that I had touched this other boy's arm when I laughed. So instead of leaving the event smiling with pride at this smart, super-fun girl he had just landed, Chad felt embarrassed by my behavior. He was embarrassed that someone thought I was more into his friend than him.

Now, I could have said, "Seriously?! I didn't even do anything. I was just talking. You have issues! You are way too sensitive!" Let me tell you why I didn't. First, I *can* be flirty at times. I'm smiley and friendly, and sometimes that can be misinterpreted by others as romantic interest. It's truly a part of my personality I have had to work on. Second—I really liked Chad. I did *not* want to make him feel like I was interested in anyone else, because I liked *him*. Third, he *was* sensitive, and I knew that. I had watched him change the channel on the TV many times before when a show broached the topic of infidelity. So instead of throwing that in his face and telling him he needed to get over it, I listened, owned my actions, and apologized. And I vowed to myself that I was going to work on this. I wanted him to know that he was safe with me.

If you have a secret, I understand the desire to keep the peace and just sweep it under the rug and forget about it. Maybe you're thinking, *Sharing this would just make things worse*, or *He's already been under so much stress lately, with his job and his mom's illness and his bad elbow. I don't want to add this to his stress. It's not worth it.* If you are thinking any version of this, you might be in danger of joining many spouses out there who have convinced themselves that they are keeping their secrets to "protect" their spouses. It's true: you don't want to hurt him or her. The problem is, you already did, and it's already affecting things, whether your spouse knows the secret itself or not. And often, the best way to make things right is to come clean.

You may read this and become convinced that I'm right. You may be thinking, *It's time to face the music and see if I can make things right—to see whether, by telling him, we can start to truly work on our marriage and make things better.* Maybe your guilt over keeping this secret has been gnawing at you for a while; maybe it's been waking you in the middle of the night. Maybe your spouse already suspects something, but you've lied so many times you can't possibly imagine 'fessing up now. Maybe you are truly worried about what will happen to her well-being, or the well-being of your kids or your family, if she learns of this.

When it comes to dealing with secrets, couples often need support. If you're unsure how to proceed or if you're worried about your spouse's well-being, seek counsel before you share your secrets. Search for a therapist, pastor, or mentor who can talk through your situation with you.

I promise, there is a light at the end of what might look like a long, dark tunnel. When you are able to confess your transgressions *without* your spouse having to learn of them elsewhere by catching you in the act, stumbling upon a text, or finding an ATM receipt, then there is hope. If *you* are the one who shares your failures with your spouse, humbly and without your beloved asking, begging, questioning, suspecting, seeking, or accusing, the process of rebuilding trust can be easier.

I have watched couples tackle even the most monumental secrets, the ones that could warrant an entire series on Lifetime, and come out on the other end stronger and more connected. Yes, the indiscretion can change everything. It can wreak havoc on a relationship. I'm not trying to sugarcoat it. However, when two people are fighting to recover, it's not uncommon for me to hear couples who are painfully working through the heartache of betrayal say, "This is so incredibly painful, but it's also the most connected we've felt in a long time."

Put this on a Post-it and frame it in your office: pain *with connection* hurts less than loneliness. I've heard it said that loneliness is the most painful human emotion. When there are secrets, which create division and harm the unity of marriage, loneliness is right around the corner.

Now, don't read this and go running to your spouse to dump twenty-five years of secrets on her while she is getting ready for bed. If you have a laundry list of secrets that could send your spouse over the edge, seek counsel. Let someone help you manage your fear and package your secrets in such a way that they can be received as well as possible, while you also give your spouse as much support as possible.

I worked for years with an array of couples who came in for intensive treatment to deal with the fallout of such a large number of secrets that, at times, they indicated an addiction—whether sexual addiction, love addiction, or pornography addiction. If your secrets involve behaviors that you believe might be linked to an addiction, find a therapist that specializes in these topics. If those behaviors have sexual links, you can look for a CSAT, a Certified Sex Addiction Therapist. You can also visit www.IITAP.com, the website for the International Institute for Trauma and Addiction, to find more information, resources, and contact information for an appropriate therapist.

We All Have Our
Own Brand of Crazy

We all have our own brand of crazy—our sensitivities, hang-ups, and vulnerabilities. Often, these vulnerabilities have some pretty solid roots. People often have extremely valid reasons why they act a certain way in certain situations. These are the reasons why a person can go from acting sane and logical to acting like a psychopath in a nanosecond. I can always tell that the sensitivities of one member of a couple are being triggered when I hear something like this:

> *Wife: I think he's bipolar!*
>
> *Me: Why do you think this?*
>
> *Wife: Because one minute everything is fine and we are just talking and calm, and then in the next minute he is freaking out and accusing me of cheating and asking who I really talked to today, and whether I really went to work. And then he starts grabbing my phone and scrolling through my call history like a maniac!*
>
> *Me (to husband): Is this how you see it?*

Husband: Well, kind of. I'm not quite sure what happened. I just know that I woke up this morning and something felt off. I had a bad dream, and then she was already gone when I woke up. She doesn't usually go to work this early. Today was different. And so I called her, and she didn't answer. And then I started to worry. I tried not to; I tried to tell myself it was fine, and she wouldn't do that do me. I tried to distract myself from that feeling, but I just couldn't shake it. When she came home, I asked her how her day was, and she said "fine" and gave short, vague responses to my questions. I asked her if she wanted to take a walk, and she said she was too tired. And then she went into the bathroom and turned on the shower, and I lost it. I ran into the room and asked her what she had really been doing, where she had really been.

Wife: Yes, it came totally out of left field. Like, what the heck? Can't a woman rest and take a shower after a hard day at work? Why does everything have to be such a big deal?

Me (to husband): What happened to you when she turned on the shower?

Husband: I don't know; I mean, I erupted. It reminded me of the time my ex-girlfriend would come home and shower immediately after work. And then one day, I saw her walking by the window, with him. Hand in hand. Laughing. They had been seeing each other for months. Right about the time when she started to come home late and was really tired at night and wanted to take a shower right away.

Like it or not, our past experiences create sensitivities in us. When those sensitivities get touched on, an almost unrecognizable, less likable version of ourselves can come out. We can look accusatory, illogical, unreasonable, dramatic, unrealistic—and often just downright crazy.

What to do about this? First, you need to know what your crazy is. And if you want to avoid a ton of confusion and misunderstandings, you may want to share it with your spouse. Of course, timing is everything. I'm not implying that you should sit on your first date and spill all your beans:

Boy: So, tell me about yourself.

Girl: Well, my dad was an abusive alcoholic who passed out drunk every night, and my mom threw him out when I was eight and I never saw him again. Therefore, I'll be extremely critical and hypersensitive to any cue that you may be lying, cheating, or stealing, and will accuse you of these things often. Oh, and due to my abandonment issues, I'll probably cry and beg you not to leave me, or I'll accuse you over and over of not really loving me. But enough about me. Tell me about you!

Why Can't I Battle My Crazy Myself?

We all have our own brand of crazy. Own yours; acknowledge it, and come together around it as a couple. Otherwise, it could cause a divide between the two of you that will spiral out of control.

There is a huge difference between couples who fight over their sensitivities and let those sensitivities divide them, and those who fight together against their sensitivities. One couple,

Melanie and Walt, came in so disconnected and sad—hanging by a thread. Melanie was sad that Walt didn't seem interested in her, didn't seem to desire her. It was like he didn't even care about her.

Melanie suffered from severe stomach pains, but you would never know it, because she would never complain. She had seen her mother complain about fictitious ailments for her entire childhood, which pushed her father away. She didn't want to be like her mother. She would never let on that she was in this kind of pain; she didn't want to look weak, and didn't want to seem like a burden. But despite her best efforts, there were times when the pain was all-consuming, forcing her to curl up in bed for hours at a time.

Walt knew she sometimes got stomachaches, but every time he asked her about her doctor's appointments, she responded, "Nope, everything looks fine. They don't know what is wrong." When she retreated to her room each night, he assumed she wanted to be alone, maybe because she was tired, or maybe even to be away from him.

At first, this couple never even mentioned the stomach pains in our sessions. Melanie had minimized them to the point that he never really thought about them. Walt did, however, wonder why she was so depressed. What had he done wrong? Why wasn't he making her happy? In an effort to avoid making it worse, and to give her what it seemed she wanted—to be alone—he let her be. They argued about how he was distant and didn't desire her, and how she was depressed and suffering because he was so distant. When it finally came out that she had severe, almost debilitating daily stomach pains, I asked, "How do you let him know you are hurting?"

She said, "I don't, really. I don't want to be a burden; he has so much to worry about as it is, I don't want to add anything to his plate. I don't want to give him more of a reason to pull away." And as she didn't want to add anything to his list of stressors, they continued to drift further apart.

Another couple, Jackson and Stacy, came to therapy because Jackson was so irritable and distant. Stacy assumed she was annoying him somehow, which was causing him to shut down. So she worked harder, tried harder, cleaned more, made better dinners, and dressed nicer. She told herself that he wouldn't be so irritable if she did *this* better and *that* better. She tried and tried, but she always fell short: he was still angry and distant.

After a few sessions, he felt comfortable enough to share that he had been physically abused as a child. He had never told a soul. When the memories haunted him at night, he would awake irritable the next morning—not because of anything she had done, but simply because of the nightmares he had every single night. She had no idea he was waking up trembling, with sweat pouring down his face, feeling like he was right back in that moment when he was a child being hurt. She had no way of knowing how to help him, no way of giving him what he needed: a cold washcloth to wipe away the sweat, the chance to be held until his body settled and calmed and he didn't feel scared any-more. She would have never known he needed a nightlight so that the room wasn't so dark, or a different painting on the wall because the one she'd picked reminded him so much of his child-hood room. She had no way to know how much it would help if she lay beside him at night while he drifted off to sleep. When he finally told her, she wept—not because she was sad for herself or their marriage, but because she was so sad for him. She was so proud, so hopeful, so honored that he had trusted her enough to tell her about his pain.

I know, I know. I can hear you already: "It's in the past. I should be over it by now. This will just make me look weak. He will just think I'm silly. What if I tell her and she doesn't even care?" Maybe you are worried about how your spouse will view you, fearful that they will see you as damaged goods. Or maybe you are worried that your past is too much of a burden, and your partner won't want to deal with it. What are they going to be able to do about it, anyway? Or maybe you are worried they will throw it back in your face: "Ah-ha! That's why you act like such a jerk, because that's how your mother treated you!" These are all sentiments I've heard time and time again as spouses wrestle with what to do with their sensitivities.

Lean into the Crazy

Whatever your and your spouse's sensitivities are, they need to be talked about, understood, and taken into account. You need to lean into each other's sensitivities and walk with each other through them. No one wants to have this conversation:

> *Wife: Oh, right. Go ahead and walk away. That's what you always do when things get tough. That's what all men do! Why should I expect anything different from you?*

> *Husband: I'm sick of it—just because your father left your mom when you were eight doesn't mean you have to take it out on me! I'm sick of getting blamed for things I didn't do!*

But when you learn to lean into each other's sensitivities, maybe she says something like this:

Wife: Here's the deal. It's not your fault. You didn't do anything to cause it, and I'm so sorry you have to bear the brunt of it. But the truth is, my dad cheated on my mom when I was eight, and because of that, I get anxious and overreactive at times. And even though it's not your responsibility to fix this for me, there are some things that I think could help me not to feel so anxious, help me not to feel like you are going to do to me what my dad did to my mom. Then, hopefully, I won't get so reactive so often. And hopefully at some point, my anxiety will go away completely. Do you think we could work on this together?

Here's another way it could go:

Husband: Here's the deal. It's not your fault your dad left your mom when you were eight and you have a hard time trusting now. I'm working really hard to make you feel safe with me. What would help the most when you get scared like that? What would help you to feel safe and trust me when you get anxious? I'm hoping I can help you in those moments. I would love for you not to feel that way at all with me someday.

Conversations can change. Take the example of the wife who never trusts that her husband is truly where he says he is or doing what he says he is doing. He texts her to say he is stopping at the grocery store on his way home, and she responds, "I don't believe you! How am I supposed to know you aren't meeting up with someone behind my back?" And he says, "I'm sick of you not trusting me! Either get over this or get out!"

I've talked before about how couples make things worse by focusing on what they *want* instead of what they *need*. Here is an example:

> *Wife: I want you to keep a GPS tracking device on you at all times, so I can check in and know where you are, and not have to worry.*

> *Husband: This is ridiculous! Do you hear how crazy that sounds? I feel like a teenage boy whose mother is trying to track him down. I'm a grown man, for goodness' sake!*

Now, here is what they *need:*

> *Wife: I know it sounds crazy, but you know I get really anxious when you change plans at the last minute. That's exactly what my dad would do: make excuses while he was really going to meet his mistress. I think what I need is your reassurance, your comfort, when I feel so anxious and scared. And sometimes, I may need you to confirm where you are. I think that would really help with my anxieties, my fears, and my ability to trust you.*

> *Husband: Of course you can trust me. I hate that this happened to you and that you have to go through this, that you don't have the luxury of being able to trust me blindly. But you can trust me. I promise. Here, listen:*

Do you hear the sound of the cash register? Would it help if we talked on the phone until I get to my car? We can just talk until your anxiety goes away.

Laying Your Pain in Their Hands

Once I get to know my couples a bit, I often start to recognize signs that there may be more to their problems than what they choose to tell me—some things in the back of their closets that they hoped they could skate through their marriage without having to divulge. When I start to see these signs, I start to work on making them feel safe enough to imagine revealing their vulnerabilities, their sensitivities, and the pain that they alone have carried from their pasts up to this point. And usually, as I work, there comes a point when I can look at them and say, "I think you may be pleasantly surprised in what your partner will say, how they will react, when you tell them this."

One of the biggest gifts you can give your spouse is to lay your pain in their hands—not to throw it directly at their face, snapping, "You know what this does to me, and you don't even care!" but rather to state, "I'm holding all this, and I don't want it to divide us, so I need to tell you about it so that you can know when it comes into play. And I really need you to handle it with kid gloves, because it was truly a painful part of my life."

❧

When two people do this and give themselves the chance to be a team, a partnership—to join together against this sad, unfortunate, sometimes horrible thing that happened and that has made such a terrible impact on them and their marriage—I just want to leap out of my therapist's chair and give them a huge hug. And a gift basket. And a parade. Because they *did it.* They shared the unimaginable, the thing one of them thought they would take to their grave. They are no longer going to suffer in silence. They are going to give their spouse the chance to *know,* to *support,* to be able to make sense of a lot of things that have not made sense—and then to *help.* Their spouse may not know exactly how to handle the information or what to do with it, but often, an amazing thing happens. The person who has drummed up the courage to reveal such an intimate part of their history may have thought their spouse would laugh at them, or look at them and say, "Ah-ha! That's why you're so crazy! I knew it! Now I'm justified in leaving you!" Instead, their spouse leans in with teary eyes and says, "I'm so sorry that happened to you." I've seen couples look like they have gained ten years on their lives when they've connected like this.

There are also couples who do know what their partners have faced. He does know that her father, who passed away when she was twelve, was mentally ill and had dementia; and that her mom was his caretaker and had little time for the rest of the family. He knows all that. He's admired his wife's strength and her resilience. But he gets so frustrated by how she tries to do everything on her own and doesn't let him help. She is used to doing it all on her own; she has since she was a little girl. But he has started to feel he can't do anything right in her eyes. And when she finally feels safe enough to talk about her past and let out some of the pain that she carries around daily—to lay it in his hands—he says, "I mean, I knew these things happened, but I had no idea they still affected her like that. I wish I knew what to do, how to help, how to take it all away."

And I say, "You are helping. By hearing her and saying what you said, you are doing just that."

Spencer and Diane struggled with sex for years and years. Spencer always felt so rejected by Diane, and by the way she turned from him when he touched her in a certain way. He would pull back, feel resentful, make sarcastic comments. In the throes of a fight, he would throw insults about what a prude she was.

After being married for eleven years and having three kids, Diane finally told him about how her uncle had sexually abused her when she was a child. And sometimes when Spencer touched her in certain ways, it would remind her of those horrible memories.

As Spencer held her and cried tears with her over what he had learned, they started to talk. They talked about what she needed in order to feel safe with him, and how they might still be able to connect physically even though she had been through so much trauma. This sweet couple was able to have many more connecting conversations about Diane's past. Over the course of these conversations, she opened up about how she felt ashamed and sad that he had to do things differently, that they couldn't just enjoy the things that other couples could. Spencer felt sad that she couldn't always find pleasure in being with him, and he wanted to do the things that made her feel safer and that would perhaps make sex enjoyable for her. Even though he cried sometimes when he was alone, and sometimes got so angry at her uncle that it kept him up at night, he no longer felt unwanted, undesired, or rejected by her. In fact, he felt needed, wanted, and connected. Sex stopped being an awful, divisive thing that caused so many arguments. Instead, it became a mission, a goal, something they worked on together.

Their success mirrored that of Walt and Melanie, who suffered from stomach pains. Once she told him how much pain she was in and how much she was suffering every day, things changed in their relationship. Her ailment actually brought them together. He started to accompany her to doctors' appointments, hold her hand as they got results and treatment plans, and tell her what she *needed* to hear: "It's going to be okay. And I'm so sorry we don't have any answers, but I'm in this with you. This isn't happening to *you*—this is happening to *us*. I am here." She came to me several sessions later rejoicing over the shift in her marriage. She felt she had gotten her husband back.

୧୬

I love the scene from *Good Will Hunting* when Robin Williams, playing the super-compassionate, persistent therapist, finally gets Matt Damon's character to talk about the fact that his father was an abusive, angry alcoholic. I have to break out the entire Kleenex box when he tells a sobbing Matt, "It's not your fault. It's not your fault that this happened to you." Over and over he says it: "It's not your fault." I seriously have a tear in my eye even thinking about this scene. Gets me every time.

It's not your fault that bad things happened to you in your past, creating these vulnerabilities, these sensitivities, these fears. But sometimes, these fears come out in ways that make us look just plain crazy. Acknowledge it. Own it. Then you and your spouse can finally do something about it. Then you and your spouse can finally admit these three important truths:

- These moments are hard for me.
- *This* is what happens to me in these moments.
- And in these moments, *this* is what I need from you. Because if you did *that*, I think it would really help. Because it came from you.

The Problem Is Not
What You Think

Therapists are masterful decoders. Sometimes I think I could moonlight for the CIA, helping decode secret languages. That's how savvy I think I've become at decoding my clients' words.

As a marriage counselor, you learn how to weed through all the arguing, accusations, ultimatums, excuses, complaints, and justifications, and get to the real root of the problem. You learn how to read between the lines, sifting through all the information about what happened last week, when a couple got into a huge fight about dog food, who left the garage door open, and why it was such a big deal that she was twenty minutes late getting home. Marriage counselors are like detectives scraping through a messy crime scene to find the one piece of DNA that will give us the culprit's identity—looking for the tiny piece of hair or particle of skin that will give us the answer to this one question: what is the root of the problem?

During an argument, a partner may only hear, "I can't believe you forgot the dog food again! You never listen to me!" Their spouse may only hear, "Oh, I listen, alright, but it's always *something* with you. You always find something to complain about!"

They are so caught up in the emotions of the fight that they can't see much of anything except that they are in distress, and that fighting with their partner is making them miserable. They don't look for the root of the problem. All they know is that emotional distance from their partner is unbearable.

As a result, my clients often want the quick fix. The answer. The solution. They lay out all the information from every angle, look at me, and ask, "What do we do?!" But I can't give you the quick fix, the perfect little communication tactic, the effective negotiation tool, because I don't know the source of the problem yet.

This much I do know: it's not about the dog food. It's not about the dishes, the garage door, or being twenty minutes late. It's about something unseen, something often unsaid, something that has escaped one spouse, if not both. And this unseen thing is different for every couple, which is why I have to go into super-sleuth mode to find it. *What is the root of the problem?*

☙

Let's look at David and Melissa. They met in graduate school in Chicago, where they later married, started their family, and moved to the suburbs to live near her mom and two sisters. Melissa found out she was pregnant with their third baby the same week David was offered a job he couldn't refuse in North Carolina. For Melissa, moving across the country was heart-wrenching, and she cried the whole way from Illinois to North Carolina.

As they entered their second year in Charlotte, the couple started to fight constantly over David's job. At first, she made little jabs and sarcastic comments about his "precious job" and his "sacred phone." When he scheduled his next work trip, she would say, "I hope you enjoy your uninterrupted sleep in your hotel room. Must be nice!" When he came home from his trip and crawled into bed, she rolled away from his embrace.

Nonetheless, David tried to make up for his time away, and jumped out of bed to help make breakfast for the kids. He took a deep breath and held his tongue when she told him, "That's what you're feeding them? Seriously? Just let me do it." He noticed her complaints about his efforts had escalated, and her nagging was at an all-time high. He told himself, *I wish she could just see how good we have it. She just likes to focus on the negative.* He recalled people in her life, like her mother, who were "the exact same way." Finally, after hearing her complain repeatedly about his efforts being wrong or not good enough, he told her, "You're so negative! Maybe you should get a hobby or a part-time job. It would do you some good to get away from the kids. We can hire a sitter a few times a week."

But having just seen David take yet another client's call during their kid's soccer game, Melissa had had it. She told him what a terrible father he was. Under her breath, she muttered, "Your clients are more important than your son."

David stewed over her insults; but in an effort not to add more fuel to the fire, he kept his mouth shut. Melissa grew more insistent, and he grew more distant.

Melissa could feel David pulling back. She sensed his distance and assumed he was depressed due to all the stress he experienced at work. She started to hate his work. *He is so selfish,* she told herself. *His priorities are so screwed up.*

David could feel Melissa becoming more and more negative. He assumed she was depressed because she had stopped working years ago so that she could stay home with the kids. He told himself, *She will be happy when she has a job again.*

When they came to therapy, they presented their arguments to me. David said Melissa was depressed and unhappy all the time, and Melissa complained that David was selfish and morally deficient. He wanted me to help her figure out how to find hobbies and friends to give her life more meaning and purpose. She wanted me to talk some sense into him, get him to see how selfish he was, and help him prioritize various aspects of his life.

⁕

The problem was, these weren't the real issues—and if a therapist treats the wrong issues, it's no different than a doctor giving you antibiotics when what you really need is surgery. Therapists can treat what the client *thinks* is the problem, put a bandage on it, or come up with amazing negotiation strategies and communication tactics. We can draw a pie chart illustrating the perfect amounts of time David needs to be spending at home or in the office. We could solicit a life coach to help Melissa find ways to enrich her life outside of being a mom. We would, however, be solving the wrong problems.

We had to look deeper. We had to peel back the layers, dissect the content, find the emotions, look for the meaning, unearth the relational need. And as we did this with David and Melissa, we learned quite a bit. We even found the culprit. Let's explore how.

When I began training in couples therapy, I started learning tactics I could use to get to the bottom of relationship problems. I was eager to apply this super-sleuthing philosophy to my own relationship. I've already shared that my husband and I had a rocky relationship when we first started dating. During that time, Chad traveled a lot for work. He also loved to play softball with a group of guys who lived forty-five minutes away. He often made plans to play in games held the night before he left for one of his three-day work trips. It really bothered me that he didn't set aside that time before he left for us—that he didn't seem to care that he would be going on a trip the day after the game. I thought that he shouldn't want to lose out on a single minute he could be spending with me before he left.

Chad, on the other hand, was utterly confused. He couldn't understand why I got upset. Why was it such a big deal that he spent one night playing softball? Who cared if it happened to fall on the night before he went out of town—especially if he had just hung out with me for three nights straight? He couldn't see my logic, and I couldn't stop my head from spinning in distress.

I started to ask myself three questions—not because I'm a remarkably insightful genius, but because I was training in Dr. Sue Johnson's amazing emotionally focused couples therapy (EFT), and her philosophy on creating and maintaining a close, healthy relationship really got me thinking. Here are the questions I asked myself:

1. What feeling is this situation bringing up for me?
2. What meaning does this situation have for me?
3. What do I really need from him?

When I slowed down and answered these questions for myself, I learned that Chad going out the night before his trips made me feel a bit sad and unimportant. I got scared that he would not make me a priority in the future. I feared that he would choose friends, activities, or jobs over me.

As it turned out, when I appropriately tuned into the situation, I realized I didn't need Chad to stay home the night before he headed out of town each week. I just needed to know that I was important to him, and that he weighed the time he spent on his outside activities against his time with me. After answering these questions, a calmness came over me. My head stopped spinning, my heart stopped pounding, and my anger stopped building. My distress made sense. When it made sense, I felt more able to handle it effectively.

After calmly sharing my distress with Chad, I started to notice his efforts to be thoughtful about his plans. When I saw him considering me, I felt I like I was a priority. At that point, it didn't matter to me whether he stayed home with me or not—I knew I was on his mind, and that I was important to him. Instead of feeling fearful, I felt reassured that he would consider me in the future. And that was all I needed to know.

Now, let's break these questions down further.

Your Feelings May Not Be What You Think

Let's talk about how to identify your feelings.

You may be thinking, *I'm super in touch with my feelings! I'm totally aware of feeling pissed, anxious, angry, resentful, frustrated, or disappointed.* Yep. You feel those things. The problem is, there's more to your emotions than what resides on the surface.

Sometimes it can be hard to identify your feelings effectively. If you are expressing and identifying your feelings over and over, but they aren't making an impact on your spouse, consider that you might not be identifying your *primary* feelings. Most likely, you are focused on your *reactive* feelings.

To use some psychological jargon, therapists learn that anger is actually a *secondary emotion*—a reaction to a deeper emotion. It's triggered when we feel hurt, unimportant, betrayed, abandoned, disconnected, misunderstood, uncared for, or unloved. If you can only identify how angry, frustrated, or resentful you are, you are missing the opportunity to find the most effective solution to your problem, one that relies on understanding the deeper emotions that triggered your anger—the core of what you are really feeling. The solution is not in the reactivity, and so it is not yet available to you. It is in the core emotion, the primary reason, the root cause.

So, how can you find the solution? Start by asking yourself, "Why am I feeling so angry? What else am I feeling? Do I feel rejected, unimportant, hurt, or something else?" Your answers will help you get to the core of the problem.

You may discover you need some help finding the answers to these questions. If you do, ask a friend, "How would you feel if someone did this to you?" Or ask yourself, "If someone did this to my daughter, son, mom, dad, or friend, how would they feel?"

Similarly, if you can only identify your emotions as anxiety, uneasiness, or being overwhelmed, you are not reaching the core of the problem. Anxiety is similar to anger, in that it is another reactive emotion: "When he leaves, I feel so much anxiety." But this isn't a deep enough understanding of the emotions derived from his absence. Instead, if you feel this way, ask yourself *why* you feel anxious: "When he leaves, I feel anxious because I start to feel _____ (disconnected, unwanted, or out of reach)." This is helpful. Let's keep going: "And when I start to feel disconnected from him, I feel _____ (scared, fearful, or lonely)."

Now we are getting somewhere! Instead of tackling the problem of his insensitivity—which is *not* the real problem—we are talking about the real problem: your fear of disconnecting from him. That fear of losing your connection to him while he is away can be truly distressing.

Now we have the root emotion—and it's not focused on

blaming your partner. It's the natural feeling that springs forward when you fear disconnection from a partner. Of *course* you feel that way! Your spouse is so important to you! You are absolutely, without a shadow of a doubt, going to have a primal, desperate, fear-based reaction to any perceived disconnect from your partner. That makes total sense!

Finding the Real Problem

Now that we know how you really feel, let's figure out what the real problem is.

This scenario has played out a thousand times in my office: Richard criticized Stephanie when she forgot to call the plumber during all her "free time." In his frustration, he accused her of being absentminded. She got defensive and gave him the laundry list of everything she had to tackle that day to keep her kids alive and fed, much less tend to his needs.

Per each other's descriptions, Richard was overbearing, with unrealistic expectations; and Stephanie was inefficient and flaky. He wanted me to come up with strategies to help her be more efficient with her time, so that she would be able to get more done and help him manage his tasks. She wanted me to help him have more realistic expectations, set the bar lower, and understand how much she had on her plate.

ജ

Watching these conversations happen in my office used to cause me great frustration. I've been the criticized wife. I've been the stay-at-home mom who forgot to run important errands because they slipped my mind after my three-year-old's seventh meltdown over losing her lovey. I've wanted to leap out of my skin and breathe fire at my husband if he implied for a second that I hadn't done a good job on the home front that day. So, during these sessions with my clients, I had to work hard to avoid making a quick judgment and become curious. And as I became curious, I was able to help couples like Richard and Stephanie peel back the layers of their emotions and find the true meaning behind their frustrations.

We had to figure out what it meant to Richard when Stephanie didn't get to the requests he made of her. We had to understand what it meant to her when he got upset at her forgetfulness.

Here's what we learned. We learned that Richard watched Stephanie handle a million tasks every day. She would do things for their neighbors, the kids, the dog, the kids' teachers, the soccer team, and the PTA—and she would reactively throw all these things in his face when he was upset. She would say, "Are you kidding me? I had to accomplish this enormous list of tasks, all while juggling the never-ending needs of our kids, and you have the nerve to complain because I forgot to call the plumber?" She would go into great detail as she described how she struggled to handle all these things, and therefore couldn't possibly do it all. She asked, "Why can't he understand that?"

Upon further sleuthing, we learned that when Stephanie spouted off the list of tasks she'd had to accomplish that day, Richard saw that she was masterfully able to handle the needs of every person in her life—except him. We learned that he felt alone and unimportant to her, with his needs the last and least important on her long list of things to do. We learned that he would tell himself, *I can't depend on her. I can only depend on me.* We learned that for Richard, a forgotten task took on a deeper meaning: it meant that he was doing life alone, instead of with his wife, whom he loved so much and who had loved him once, too, he thought, even if it felt like a long time ago. And this made him feel truly sad.

We also learned a few things about her. We learned that when Richard got angry with her and insulted her competence, she not only felt angry ("How dare he! Can't he see all I'm doing?"), but also incredibly sad. Sad that she was letting him down; that despite her best efforts, she was getting it wrong. She started to fear that she wasn't the right partner for him, that he needed someone who was more organized and efficient. She feared he didn't want her. We learned that for her, the problem wasn't Richard's high expectations—it was her fear that he wanted someone else, someone different. And this thought made her cry at night after he fell asleep.

Now we were getting somewhere. We discovered the meaning behind their fights. We understood that the root problems for him were his fear of being alone in life and the feeling that he couldn't depend on her. We learned that the root problem for her was the overwhelming fear that she might not be the right partner for him, that she might not be who he wanted—even though she desperately wanted to be.

Now we have the appropriate diagnosis. Let's keep digging.

One of the most common pitfalls a person faces in working through their dissatisfactions in their relationship is blaming their partner for their discomfort, accusing their partner of being the cause of their dissatisfaction. They think their partner is the problem, and therefore, changing him or her is the solution. But if this is your view of your marriage, you are sending the wrong person to jail. For life.

Instead, the problem lies in the dynamic, in the way two partners interact with each other. We need to focus on the real problem. Moreover, the problem is not the discomfort. The discomfort is expected when there is perceived distance, misunderstanding, conflict. The discomfort appropriately informs us that something is off, and that we have a relational need that is getting missed. The discomfort is helpful. It's an alarm, a red flag, a nudge letting us know that something is needed here. What is not helpful, though, is taking that discomfort and convincing yourself or your partner that he or she is fully responsible for the pain you're in. The discomfort is not the problem, but merely a sign, a suggestion, that you need your partner. However, what you *do* with this discomfort might make all the difference between coming together as a couple and creating further distance.

I've decided that all my masterful decoding skills can be put to good use. Surely others could benefit from all I've learned while engaging in complex problem-solving between two partners. So I created a cheat sheet. You will see the perceived problem, the one that seems obvious to a partner. And you will see the real problem, the more hidden but amazingly powerful root. In giving you this cheat sheet, I'm hoping that with its help, you can skip over the years of frustrating, never-ending problem-solving tactics and just go right to the root.

What's the Real Problem—A Cheat Sheet

You are insensitive. *It hurts me when it seems you don't think about me, because you are the person I care about most.*

You are selfish. *Sometimes, it feels like I'm alone, doing things by myself—which is very painful and sad, because I want to be going through life with you, more than anyone else in the world.*

You are lazy. *I'm so overwhelmed with trying to do so much. I feel like I'm drowning in all the demands that have been placed on me. I want to feel like I'm by your side, not alone. It means the world to me to know we are in this together as partners.*

You are damaged. Something is wrong with you. *The distance between us causes me so much distress, and I'm scared that you don't care enough about me to give me what I need to feel close to you. The pain of not feeling close to you is unbearable.*

You are way too uptight. *I watch you work so hard for the kids, the school, your job, and our neighbors, and I see how it affects you. At times, you seem so overwhelmed and stressed by it all that I can't seem to find a place in your life. I feel like all this stress gets between us, which makes me feel sad and lonely.*

You need to work on your anxiety/depression. Maybe you should see a therapist. *Sometimes, I don't know how to reach you when you seem anxious or depressed. I'm trying everything I know in order to help, but I'm at a loss. And the reason I care so much is because I feel so distant from you during those times. The reason I make suggestions like getting on medication and going to a therapist is because I'm hoping that doing those things could help you feel better, which I hope will ultimately help me feel close to you again. That's what I truly want. It is the most helpless feeling in the world* to feel like I can't improve this aspect of your life, and sometimes when I try to do it anyway, the methods I try only make you feel worse. I am so sad about that. I would love to go to therapy together to see if we can make changes in our relationship, or if I can make changes that would help.

You are a workaholic. Or an alcoholic. Or a technology addict. *It hurts me to watch you turn to everything but me for your comfort. I truly feel like I'm competing with your work, a drink, your phone, your computer. I want to be your comfort—but I feel like I'm losing to the competition, and that leaves me feeling incredibly sad and alone. I'm desperate for you to turn to me.*

You are a sociopath. You have no emotions. *I'm struggling with feeling pushed away. I can't seem to reach you. I know there is a depth to you to which I'm not privy. I know it may be out of your comfort zone to talk about certain things, but I struggle with the feeling that I'm not getting the true you, which is something I really want. It makes me feel very alone when I'm not let into your inner world.*

You are an a*$%hole / b#@ch. *You have hurt me, and the reason this thing you did or said hurts so much is because I care so much about you and our relationship. You can hurt me worse than anyone else can, because I care more about you than I do about anyone else. I'm trying to get your attention by calling you names and throwing insults at you, because what I really need is your comfort, your apology, your genuine and sincere words expressing your regret. Even though you are the one who hurt me, you are the one who has the power to help me most.*

You are coming home late—again! *I miss you, and so do the kids, because we love you.*

You are so unappreciative of how hard I work! *I'm so torn between my need to provide for our family and my need to be present for the family. I'm not sure how to reconcile those needs, but I think it would help to feel like you understand my struggle and how important it is to me to provide for us.*

You don't care about me. You don't act like you love me. *Our dynamic leaves me feeling distant, sad and lonely. Do you feel that way sometimes, too? I think we are both doing things that create distance between us. Can we talk about ways to reconnect so I can feel cared for and loved in our marriage? What do you need from me in order to feel more loved and cared for?*

Finding the Right Answer

Now that we have grasped the real problem, we can look for the right answer.

Couples always want this answer ASAP—like, yesterday. "Just tell me what to do already! My marriage is deteriorating into nothing! We can't take it anymore! Give us the answer, Lori!"

Okay, okay. Since you have identified your true feelings and thought long and hard about the true meaning of your struggles, you are ready for the answer. The answer lies in learning what your relational needs are, what your partner's needs are, and how to ask your partner to fulfill your needs in a way that makes it easy for them to want to do so.

These needs are different for every couple, for every partner. I can't be immediately certain what you or your partner needs to feel happy, safe, and secure in your relationship. But thanks to the researchers like Dr. Sue Johnson and Drs. John and Julie Gottman, who have invested their careers in studying couples and relationships, I have a pretty good guess. I just need your help in finding out exactly what those needs are for you.

Based on her compelling research, Dr. Johnson has identified what people need to feel secure and loved in their intimate relationships: connection, comfort, reassurance, acceptance, safety. They need to feel wanted, needed, desired, important, heard, and respected. They need to know they can count on their partner to be there for them.

Try remembering your thoughts after your last fight or disappointment. You may have thought, *It would be so nice if he or she would just* _____ *(listen, understand, appreciate, validate, reassure me, reach out to comfort me, take time to connect with me, desire me, want me, care about me).* Think about these one by one as you consider the content of your fight. Which one resonates?

Now we are getting to a resolution. We know your core feelings, the real meaning behind this fight for you and your partner, and what you really need in order to be happy—the types of needs that, when met, transform relationships. The types of needs that, when expressed in a vulnerable and loving way, can elicit a vulnerable and loving response. When you have taken the time to identify your feelings and the meaning behind your distress, you are much better equipped to tackle your relational needs in an effective manner. If you ask for your needs in ineffective ways, do not be surprised when they are not met.

To be clear, you should not hurl your needs at your spouse amid insults such as, "You are such an a@%—you know I need your support right now! How can you be so dumb?" You also shouldn't be mixing your explanations of your needs with comments about your lack of faith in your spouse's abilities, like so: "I just wish for *once* you could listen to me and validate me. You are *never* there for me when I need you!"

Instead, you should let your partner know your primary feelings, the meaning you attribute to this situation in your relationship, and the deep desire you have for them to meet your specific need. Instead of accusing or attacking them, you should say, "I'm so sad and scared. I've noticed a change in our relationship; we seem more distant, we are arguing more often, we don't seem to talk the way we used to. Our distance makes me scared that we are drifting away from each other. I'm so sad when I feel far from you. I want to feel close to you right now. And I think it would help if you gave me a hug and reassured me it's going to be okay. I think it would also help if we spent some time together tonight. Maybe we could get a sitter this weekend, too. Would that be okay with you?" And now we have the answer.

Let's take a look back at David and Melissa. Once we peeled back its layers, we learned their fight had different meanings for each of them, based on what they had faced in their pasts.

When Melissa was growing up, her father had often been absent. He traveled for work for weeks at a time—until one day, he left Melissa's mother and started a new family with another woman.

Melissa had done her best to cope with her feelings of abandonment while she comforted her brokenhearted mom. She promised herself her children would never have an absent father. When she met David, he treated her like gold. She recalled thinking when she'd married him how grateful she was to have found a husband so unlike her father.

When David and Melissa were dating during graduate school, they spent late nights studying together. David recalled that when he'd proposed to Melissa, he had felt incredibly grateful that she was as driven as he was. They were both rapidly climbing the corporate ladder when Melissa became pregnant with their first child. When she fell pregnant with their second, David supported her decision to take some time off from her stressful job and stay home with the kids while he acted as the sole breadwinner.

As our sessions continued, we learned that when David had begun spending more and more time at the office, Melissa's feelings of abandonment became so strong, she almost couldn't contain them. She wanted to do everything short of tracking David down and sending out Navy SEALs to bring him home in order to relieve the panic she felt. We learned that when she got scared like that, she needed to know she was important to him—more important than his work.

During our sessions, we learned about David as well. We learned that he had been raised by an extremely successful father, who in turn came from a long line of successful men. When David was a child, his father had used every opportunity to remind David of the expectations his name bestowed upon him. David recalled the shame he'd felt when his father expressed disappointment in him, whether it was because he had brought home an A- or pitched a losing baseball game. As a result, David worked hard to make the grade, to make the team, to win the game—anything to avoid his father's disapproval.

We learned that when Melissa made her sarcastic jabs at his job or gave him a disappointed look after he missed a family dinner, David felt the same sense of shame and failure he had experienced when his father rebuked him. He was in constant turmoil, feeling that no matter what he did, he would be failing either his father or his wife. We learned that he needed her to understand that he wasn't amoral, but instead fiercely afraid that he would simultaneously let down both of his loved ones. We learned that he lay in bed at night talking himself out of his feeling of panic. Would he be the first failure in his family? What if he couldn't give his wife and kids the life he'd had? Who would he be then?

When David and Melissa learned of their own and each other's core emotions, and understood their relational needs and the meaning these fights had for themselves and each other, amazing things happened. Melissa was able to say, "I understand your desire to please everyone, including me, and that in doing so, you are burning the wick at both ends. I can't imagine how scary it is to be our sole provider. I see how much you care about our family—so much so that you are working yourself to the bone. Let me be in this with you. If I can be privy to your turmoil, I'll feel close to you, which will make all this chaos bearable. I want to support you; I just need extra reassurance and connection, especially when you are away. I can't handle the burdens of home life and the kids and also feel disconnected from you. For me to endure this season of our lives, I need to feel like you are in it with me."

For his part, David was able to say, "I want to lessen the toll on you when I'm away. I never want you to feel scared that you aren't important to me. I know you must feel that way sometimes thanks to my long workdays. I don't ever want you to question your importance, or worry I won't be here for you. I want to make sure that even if I'm not here with you and the kids physically, you can lean on me emotionally. I need to do that better. I need to put down my computer at night and stop checking emails on my phone after hours. I really do want to be here for you. It would mean the world to me if I also knew that you see how hard I work for our family, and that you understand my motivations. I think if I felt more understood by you, I wouldn't be so defensive when you come to me for comfort. I think I can even use your support in helping me find more balance in my life. Sometimes I get so overwhelmed, I just fall into go-mode. I would love for you to work with me to help me shut it off."

By the close of our many sessions, David and Melissa had learned to lean into each other. Each had discovered a genuine desire to meet the other's needs. And their relationship grew all the better for it.

You may wonder how things got resolved with Richard and Stephanie. In a pivotal moment of vulnerability, Stephanie bravely shared her feelings with Richard and told him that she cried herself to sleep at night at the thought of not being what he wanted. I asked Richard how he felt about her words, and this was his reply:

Richard: Important.

Me: Can you say more?

Richard: If she's that upset at the thought of not being enough for me, I can't doubt how important I am to her.

Richard later told me that, knowing how important he was to Stephanie, he stopped caring when she forgot to do something he asked. He knew that her forgetfulness only meant she had been busy tending to their amazing family. It stopped meaning that he wasn't important to her.

I also noticed a change in Stephanie. In another pivotal

moment, as Richard shared his sadness at feeling alone and unimportant to her, Stephanie leaned forward in her chair. I asked her how she felt about his words, and this was her reply:

Stephanie: Wanted.

Me: Can you say more?

Stephanie: If feeling unimportant to me makes him that sad, I have no doubt that he wants me.

When Stephanie felt wanted, she no longer crumbled when Richard said, "Did you remember to buy more dog food?" Instead, she would reply with humor: "Nope! But I kept the kids alive and fed today. I call that a win!"

I also noticed a few more changes. So as not to make her feel unwanted, Richard softened his critiques of Stephanie. For her part, Stephanie made efforts to remind Richard of his importance to her, and picked up his favorite coffee or ice cream at the store. Together, these little attentions started to make a huge difference in their relationship.

❧

I'll end with this example. I was once asked to be a part of the wedding of a dear friend of mine. She had a short engagement, and her list of out-of-town wedding activities and plans almost gave me a panic attack. I wanted her to hear my laundry list of extremely valid reasons why I wouldn't be able to attend all her nuptial engagements.

As I thought about telling her I couldn't make it to everything, I started to feel angry. Shouldn't she have known I had a crazy busy life with my kids, and couldn't possibly do all these fun things with her?

This is often where my clients are when they come in to see me—stuck at this stage, angry and feeling justified in their positions. But I recognized this, and used the previously described strategies to analyze the problem I was having with my friend. I realized that underneath my anger, I felt scared. I was worried that if I couldn't do all the activities my friend had planned, I would disappoint her. I was worried she would think our friendship wasn't important to me, and that she wasn't important to me. I learned that what my emotions really meant for me was that she was a dear, dear friend, and the thought that she wasn't important to me was the last thing I wanted her to feel. That thought did not make me angry at all. Actually, it made me really sad.

I fretted about what to do, about how to solve this complex problem! I thought about each of our needs in this situation. I needed her compassion and understanding of my limitations. She needed my reassurance that despite my chaotic life, she was important to me, and I was going to do everything in my power to give her the time I could during this very special period in her life.

After all my introspection, I was calmly able to call her. I didn't have a plan of negotiation for how to split my time. I didn't have a way to apply better time management skills. I just had my feelings, the core meaning, an understanding of my needs and my desire to meet hers. When we spoke, I simply shared with her that I was scared. I was scared that my limitations were going to disappoint her and make her feel unimportant, and that thought made me very sad. It was the last thing I wanted. I wanted to reassure her of her importance (her need) while also asking for her compassion and understanding (my need).

We talked and shared and laughed and came up with a creative solution we both felt good about. But even after that, I'm sure she was still a little disappointed about the things I was going to miss, and I was a little sad knowing I was letting her down. We couldn't fix it all. We couldn't erase every potential downfall. But we got through this super-sensitive situation with our relationship fully intact, and without any disruption to the power of our friendship. We still had some complex feelings, some unresolvable problems, but we still had the strength of our connection. And *that* is the solution.

It takes a lot of insight, reflection, and digging down deep to be able to recognize, "The reason I'm so mad at you is because I care so much about what you think that I'm terrified of letting you down. I'm scared that something I do might come between us—and I don't want that, because I love you so much."

The Truth About
Disconnection

In my experience as a marriage counselor, there are two popularly stated reasons that couples come in for therapy. One is "We need to learn how to communicate," and the second is "We are disconnected."

I've already spent quite a bit of time addressing the problem of communication, but now I want to spend some time addressing the problem of disconnection.

As I explore this topic with a couple, I often hear the following reasons for their disconnect: "We don't talk anymore." "We don't have common interests." "We are so caught up with the kids we hardly make time for each other anymore." "We are too tired and busy for sex." "We have just grown apart." And finally—"We are just two different people now. We've changed since we got married."

As two spouses talk about these reasons, both of them eagerly nod in agreement. "Yep," they say, "this is the story. This is how it happened. We had kids, got busy, stopped making time for each other, started to enjoy different things, and ultimately grew apart." As they explain their story of disconnection to me, they are often at the chapter of resignation. One or both has accepted the seeming reality that they have grown apart, and believe there is not much that can be done now.

There are so many resources available when it comes to marriage. The shelf in the self-help section of the bookstore is overcrowded with books offering advice on marriage—books just like this one. I find daily posts and articles on marriage in renowned magazines, or on news sites, social media, and blogs. Advice on how to connect with a partner is everywhere. You can log into Twitter or Facebook and find someone sharing "steps to a healthy marriage" every day.

Usually, couples are aware of these strategies. They understand that wanting connection means they should go on date nights, make time for each other, listen to each other, compliment each other, make their marriage a priority, express appreciation for each other, make time for sex, and get off their phones and iPads when they are together. They are not coming to couples therapy to learn these things. They can find them with a quick Google search.

However, despite having all this knowledge, couples can often feel quite hopeless. They know all this, but they aren't doing it. Neither spouse is making the marriage a priority or taking the time to hear each other; they aren't going on date nights or having sex anymore. They aren't putting down their phones at night or turning off the TV to talk. It's not that they don't understand that they should be spending quality time with their spouse in order to feel connected. It's not that they don't get that they should be having sex periodically instead of going into separate rooms at night after the kids are in bed. It's not because they are lazy. It's not because they don't care. It's not because she likes to watch reality TV and he likes to watch baseball. Contrary to popular belief, TV preferences did not ultimately cause their disconnect.

Are You Disconnected or Hurt?

Often, the true reason for the disconnect is that these spouses are hurt. Usually, when such a couple comes into my office, it doesn't take long for me to discover that they have experienced weeks, months, and years of hurt piled on top of hurt. And when a partner is weighed down by hurt, they aren't entirely motivated to incorporate all these connecting strategies into their marriage. These hurts have created a lot of pain, and couples don't know how to stop the pain. They don't have a lot of hope that date nights, incorporating weekly sex, pursuing a shared hobby, or watching the same TV shows is going to heal the pain of the hurts. They have gotten to the point that it seems the only reasonable way out of this pain is separation.

Disconnection is often the code word for hurt. People feel much less vulnerable saying, "I feel disconnected," than they do saying, "I feel hurt." It feels too risky, too frightening, too revealing to say to a partner, "I feel alone, ignored, hurt, rejected, invisible." Instead they say, "We are just so disconnected—don't you agree?" In therapy, they look at me as they explain their story, waiting for me to nod and say, "Oh, yes, of course. It looks like you just grew apart naturally and gradually. There's really not much that can be done at this point. You truly are two different people who have changed since you were married. It happens to the best of us."

Now, plenty of couples who come in "disconnected" are not planning to separate. They report their frustration and discontent with the disconnect. If they haven't fully resigned themselves to this disconnection as their final fate in this marriage, they tell themselves that it's just a phase. They have hope that after this phase of life—when the kids get a bit older, and they start getting a bit more sleep and have more free time—they will start to connect again. Maybe when they aren't so exhausted from chasing around little ones or running to five million extracurricular activities, they'll stay up together and talk, spending quality time together like they used to instead of passing out on the couch by 9:15 p.m. Maybe then they won't feel so lonely.

Don't get me wrong—I daydream about the day that my husband and I will be able to have a full conversation without constant interruptions. I cannot wait to sit on our back patio, sipping lemonade and talking about our days without having to jump up and push a swing or decide whose turn it is to play with the sandbox truck.

I'm sure (please let it be so) it will be easier to have time together and feel connected as the kids get older. However, as I am currently immersed in this chaotic time of life, I believe that connection should still exist. Yes, it's insanity; yes, it's hard; yes, the kids drive us crazy. But we are a team. We acknowledge the chaos, daydream together about the days when it gets easier, and reminisce together about our pre-child days when we galivanted all over the globe without a worry in the world.

There still needs to be connection during the chaos. And it's absolutely possible.

I see a lot of couples who come to therapy *after* all the chaos has ended. The kids are graduating, leaving for college, going off to join the military, or starting their first jobs at a firm in DC. These couples have finally reached a point when they have all the time in the world for each other. Unfortunately, for some, it feels too late. They look at their partner as a stranger, the shadow of someone they used to know and love. They are now deciding whether to reengage in a relationship that feels uncertain, or to move on.

As I watch these couples struggle with this decision, as they wonder whether there is any sort of spark of connection left with which to salvage this marriage, I think to myself, *How did they get here?*

Why I Hate the Word "Disconnection"

In couples therapy, the word "disconnected" reveals very little, to me or to couples. For some spouses, hearing that their partner feels disconnected is about as alarming as hearing that they have a sensitive tooth: it doesn't necessarily make an impact or motivate them to change. It does not imply, "Emergency! Call a medic!" More often it implies, "Darn, this tooth again. I guess I'll call a dentist and get it looked at in the next couple of months or so." Having a sensitive tooth is annoying, uncomfortable, and undesirable, and of course you'd prefer not to have it, but surely you can manage in spite of it.

In reality, a feeling of disconnection from the person that matters most in our lives can bring up the same emotions we experience in a life-threatening situation: panic, fear, despair and loneliness. But if you use only mildly alarming words to describe those emotions, you'll probably get only a mild response.

In sessions, I have seen conversations about a couple's disconnection look like this:

Wife: We are so disconnected.

Husband: I guess so. We are just so busy, though.

Wife: I know, but we need to make time together.

Husband: Okay, we can spend more time together;

that's fine.

Wife: Okay.

Me: Are we good? Are we done? Is that all you needed?

Wife: No . . .

Husband: Yes, I think we're good. We can just start spending more time together. That should solve it.

Wife: Well . . . I'm sure that will help, but I don't know if it will help enough.

Husband: Okay . . . ummmm . . . what else do you want?

Wife: I don't know—maybe if we started going to bed at the same time?

Husband: Sure, that's fine. We can give that a try. (to me): I think we are good here. How much do we owe you?

Wife: No, we aren't done. I just want to make sure we are fully connected.

Husband (through gritted teeth): Okay, what else do you want?

To me, this conversation is a bit like pulling teeth (yes, I'm really sticking to my tooth metaphor). They are talking in circles about this abstract concept of disconnection. They are trying to put little bandages on a gaping wound, or even pretending that this gaping wound doesn't exist. And usually, there is a very confused spouse in the midst of this, a spouse who hears all about this alleged disconnection, but who has no earthly idea what it means or how to solve it. But spending a bit more time together and planning the occasional date night should do the trick—right?

I agree with this confused spouse. I too have no idea what the elusive idea of "disconnection" means to their partner specifically. So I try to poke around and figure out exactly what they are experiencing that is leaving them feeling so disconnected. As I poke around, I usually land on that gaping wound—the one that has never healed, and that often gets reinjured over and over again. Ah-ha! It's not that the confused spouse is disconnected—it's that they are hurt. For a litany of potential reasons, they have not been able to find repair, relief, or comfort in their partner to heal this hurt. Therefore, they have turned to many other methods for relief: TV, the kids, busyness, exercise, work, alcohol, confiding in another, etc. And as they turn to these methods instead of to their partner to find relief from the pain over and over again, they widen the divide between them and their spouse, compounding the hurt.

Through all the chaos, partners either find comfort in each other, or they find comfort elsewhere. When they find comfort elsewhere instead of turning to their partner, they create hurt.

I think a more accurate way to describe the feeling of disconnection might be, "I have a lot of pain, whether that pain is caused by my partner or not, and I am unable to find comfort for this pain in my partner, and that leaves me in a lot of distress." Or, "My partner doesn't come to me to find comfort. He turns to everything else instead of coming to me, and that leaves me in a lot of distress." For many couples, the inability to find comfort from pain in a partner is one of the primary reasons for disconnection, separation, and divorce.

The Antidote to Disconnection

If disconnection is a marriage-killer, comfort is the antidote. When a couple learn how to use each other as a place of comfort, relief, and refuge from the pain caused within and outside their marriage, disconnection doesn't stand a chance. Any perceived disconnection is erased and rectified by a comforting experience: the experience of sharing your pain and finding relief in your partner's response. When a couple learn to do this, they have this amazing restorative power at their fingertips. They can activate this power to restore connection at any point, regardless of what life throws at them.

The ability to take your distress, pain, hurts, and discomfort to your partner and experience validation, understanding, relief, and comfort is the cornerstone of a strong attachment. Dr. Johnson's renowned research confirms the power of this experience. As she and her team observed thousands of couples, they concluded that the ability to find comfort in your partner is the most important part of a relationship. It is more important than stellar communication skills, more important than sexual expertise, more important than learning how to negotiate and compromise. The research was so compelling that it led her to create emotionally focused couples therapy (EFT), a therapy model that focuses intently on helping couples learn and practice the skill of getting and giving comfort in their marriages.[2] When couples can find comfort in each other, they can conquer a wide range of other conflicts, like parenting, sex, communication, and differing interests. In short, the ability to find comfort in your partner and vice versa creates the foundation of a

---

2. For more information regarding emotionally focused couples therapy or Dr. Susan Johnson, visit www.ICEEFT.com. Dr. Johnson's groundbreaking book *Hold Me Tight: Seven Conversations for a Lifetime of Love* is a must-read for every married couple.

relationship. When a relationship has this kind of secure footing underneath it, a couple can weather the storms of chaos.

The outcomes research on EFT therapy indicates that it is a remarkable success. In couples therapy, it leads me to quickly home in on the presence, or lack, of comfort in a relationship. I ask, "Do you seek out your spouse for comfort? How do you let your spouse know that you need them? Does your spouse seek you out for comfort? How do you comfort your spouse when they are hurting?" And I ask, "How do they let you know they are hurting?"

Most often, couples fall into one of three categories. Some can recall a time when they used to be a place of comfort for each other. They can describe experiencing moments of comfort and connection between themselves when they were dating, or at critical points in their relationship—for example, when a loved one died, when she had a miscarriage, when they were having difficulty conceiving, or when he was experiencing trouble with his extended family. They can describe their experience of feeling pain, seeking comfort, and receiving comfort in their partner. In these types of critical moments, they can find their partner. However, they often report, when the source of the pain is their partner, they have not been able to find comfort in each other. They feel comfortable in taking outside stressors to their spouse, but when their spouse *is* the stressor, they don't. Usually, they have little confidence that bringing up their relational distress to their partner will elicit a loving, caring, and comforting response.

Some couples can recall experiences in seeking comfort in each other no matter the cause. They have experienced finding comfort in their relationship regardless of whether their coworker or their spouse caused the pain. The problem is that these experiences were in the past. For a variety of reasons, such as a crisis or a series of difficult life events, their partner is no longer a place of comfort, and they haven't felt the healing and connecting power of this experience in quite some time. For some, the crisis is a betrayal of trust, and the partner they thought they trusted for comfort no longer feels like a safe place.

Finally, there are the couples who have never viewed each other as a true place of comfort. Typically, these spouses have limited experience finding comfort in people. They are more likely to internalize, ruminate, compartmentalize, isolate themselves, and turn to other avenues for comfort. Often, these people learned to rely on themselves at an early age. They never learned how to share painful emotions, or never deemed it safe to do so. Instead, they learned to find comfort in ways that do not require vulnerability, seeking relief in work, alcohol, sex, pornography, gambling, affairs, exercise, hobbies, volunteer work, social events, friendships, their children—the list goes on and on. Basically, they seek comfort *everywhere*—in healthy or unhealthy places—*except from their spouse.*

Sometimes, this drives a marriage to a slow death. While this couple may never have experienced the level of true intimacy that is possible when partners are able to be vulnerable with each other, they have managed to create fun times and feelings of companionship. They have had success co-parenting, and building family memories without seeking comfort in each other. For other couples, the absence of this vulnerability is a gaping hole that can't possibly be ignored—one that causes the marriage to crumble in an instant when a life event finally shines a spotlight on it.

Often, couples come to therapy with laundry lists of gripes

and complaints about each other. They want to talk in great detail about their different parenting styles, their contrasting approaches to disciplining their four-year-old, their nonexistent sex life, and their disagreements on whether the bed should be made every morning and the dishes washed before bed every night. All these experiences are valid and frustrating, and all cause distress. However, if we dive into solving these issues without learning how to seek and receive comfort in a partner, the marriage will continue to struggle. We might make some short-term progress, but the long-term problem will typically come creeping back.

Healthy couples find comfort in each other when they feel pain. In fact, for each member of a healthy couple, their partner is their go-to person. They have an immediate urge to seek out their spouse for comfort when pain shows up. They are champing at the bit for the day to end, for the meetings to stop, for the phone to quiet down, and for the kids to get to bed, so that they can finally take their stress, hurt, and pain to their partner. They are eager to feel the relief the connection with their partner offers them.

Distressed couples do not find comfort in each other when they feel pain. They turn to everything and anything except their spouse.

I am not implying that your spouse should be your only source of comfort. There are many healthy ways to find relief from pain, and in a healthy marriage, partners can use all sorts of ways. Emotionally safe friends and family members, prayer, exercise, meditation, mindfulness, socialization, work success, rest, hobbies, fun, quiet time, harmless distractions such as reading a thriller or watching a funny TV show, and spending time with the kids can all be healthy ways to experience relief and comfort. The key is that your partner should also be on this list. Your partner needs to be one of many comforting places you can turn to with your pain. If you are not turning to your partner for comfort in effective ways, or if you are not receiving an effective response, expect disconnection to creep into the marriage and eventually—possibly—take over.

If you recognize that you and your spouse are not finding comfort in each other, you have just identified a key weakness in your marriage. This is a great start!

As you work to decide your next step, it may be helpful to ask yourself a few questions. Some couples can sort out this process together. Others need a bit more help, and may require the guidance of a skilled marriage counselor. If you're ready to move on to the next step, first ask these questions of yourself and your spouse:

1. What keeps me from turning to my spouse for comfort? What keeps my spouse from turning to me for comfort?
2. Have we been a source of comfort to each other in the past? What did this look like? Can I identify when that changed?
3. Can I imagine finding comfort in my partner? What would that look like? Can I imagine giving my partner comfort? What would this look like?
4. Am I willing to talk to my partner about wanting to create this experience between us?
5. Do I have hope that if we talk about this together, we can talk about it effectively?

As I help couples either create or restore the ability to find comfort in each other, I have noticed a few things. For some, it's like riding a bike. If they have had this experience in the past, the ability to create it again can come rushing back with some honest conversations. They can talk openly about their answers to the questions listed previously and get themselves back on track. They can talk honestly about what changed for them emotionally and when. They can be open to hearing about specific hurts that may have caused this shift, and be willing to repair the hurts. They can talk candidly about their emotional needs, and about what they can do in order to feel emotionally safe with each other again.

However, if their answer to question 4 or 5 is "no," it may be time for the couple to consider seeking out a marriage counselor. If the state of their relationship is such that they cannot even imagine having these types of conversations with their spouse in an effective way, it may be wise to solicit help. Often, if one or both partners has not experienced people or their partner as a safe place for comfort, or if there has been betrayal in the relationship, the thought of doing this can feel terrifying. In fact, partners can describe their fear of opening up to their partner in a vulnerable way as akin to their fear of jumping off a cliff—they are that afraid or unsure that their spouse will be a safe place for their more vulnerable emotions to land.

I've also noticed that some partners constantly gauge whether their spouse is a good place to seek out comfort. They tune into their spouse's body language, gestures, and tone of voice. They recognize any perceived disinterest or annoyance in their partner's response to what they say. They can notice their partner quickly glance at their phone or check the time, and interpret this as complete indifference to their pain. They can decide in seconds that their partner is not a safe, open, and loving place to take their pain. They make assumptions in an instant, thinking, *He doesn't care about this,* or *She is too busy for this,* or *She wants me to be strong and have it all together,* or *He doesn't want to see me appear weak.*

Partners are often so sensitive to their spouses' feelings and actions. They can take one or two instances of perceived inattention on the part of their partner and decide, *Nope, it's not safe to take my problems to that person. They don't care; they don't want to know. They can't handle it. I need to figure this out on my own.*

I remember a couple who came to therapy in their seventeenth year of marriage. As we explored their disconnection, he recalled an experience that had occurred early in their marriage. He recalled that he had broken down in tears, and she'd told him to "man up." He'd decided in that moment that he would never take his pain to her again, and he didn't . . . until he came to couples therapy all these years later.

I remember a couple who came in to therapy because the husband appeared extremely distant. His wife couldn't figure out what was wrong; she'd begun to wonder whether he was depressed. With some prompting from me, he started to open up in session about the pressures he was under and how overwhelmed he felt. After listening for a bit, she looked at him with pained eyes and asked, "Why wouldn't you tell me this? Why wouldn't you let me help you with this?"

He responded, "I tried to talk to you about it, remember? I told you that one morning at the breakfast table, and you told me not to make such a big deal of it."

Of course, she didn't remember being dismissive. But this is often how disconnection happens: one partner feels hurt at the perceived dismissiveness of the other. And from then on, they decide they will deal with their pain on their own.

There could be a thousand reasons why a couple might not seek comfort in each other. For some, it seriously has not even crossed their minds. At some point, they received the message that difficult emotions are meant to be repressed, or dealt with privately. They haven't looked at their partner as someone who can, should, or would even know how to help.

When I counsel individuals, they pour out their pain and hurts. When I ask how they share these hurts with their spouse, they look bewilderedly at me. "I guess I don't," they say. Often their spouse's only clue that they are struggling is their short temper, their quietness, their irritability, or their lack of patience. Very rarely do these behaviors send the message, "I'm hurting," or "I need you." Very rarely do these behaviors elicit a compassionate, loving, and comforting response.

✧

Often, a spouse does not see their partner as capable of handling painful feelings. For example, a wife may know that her husband has difficulty expressing his own painful emotions or talking with his wife about hers. He may even have perfected the ability to avoid all pain—both his and his wife's.

This wife wants a solution. She wants her husband to give her emotional support. But instead, her reactions to his "incapability" of being there for her when she is in distress often further incapacitates him. If this wife feels pain and does not feel she's getting the support she needs, she may react with anger, criticism, and accusations directed at her "oblivious" husband. In turn, he sees her anger as further evidence of his inadequacies.

Angry and hurt, he continues to try to avoid exposing his inadequacies, which usually means he avoids talking about her emotions altogether. He doesn't want to keep messing up.

Here is some insider info on marriage counseling. Marriage counselors spend every minute of each session, every tool in their tool bag, and every tactic they know to help couples turn to each other with their pain and say these simple words: "I'm hurting," and "I need you." And then, we pull out every stop to help the partner lean in and say, "I see your hurt. You can come to me. I am here for you." And then we help couples do this over and over again, until it becomes routine and familiar. Until couples can't even imagine doing it any other way. This way feels too good. They never want to go back to how it was before. And then, our work is done.

When It Comes to Sex, You Are Both Right

There is a good reason I saved the sex conversation for the end. It's not because it's the least important. (Actually, it could easily have been Chapter Two or Three.) It's because I downright dreaded writing it.

Here's an interesting confession: I'm a marriage counselor who used to dread talking about sex. We never talked about it in my home while I was growing up, and I've had to work really hard to get comfortable talking about it now. Blame my super-Southern roots; blame my parents; blame society; blame the church. Blame whoever, but the truth is, talking about sex openly has been a struggle for me. The thought of my parents or in-laws reading this chapter makes me want to crawl in a hole and hide for ten years.

I say this to prove that sometimes, it's hard to talk about sex in a meaningful way. But as marriage counselors everywhere will tell you, you *have* to talk about sex in your marriage. You *have* to talk—about your needs, your desires, your wants, what feels good, what you like, what they like, and so on and so forth. *Eeek!*

It's so strange that even though we have shared this level of intimacy with our spouses on many occasions—and often even have a couple of kids to show for it!—it still can feel awkward. Before I became a marriage counselor, I would rather have poked my eyes out than talked about sex. So if it is hard for you, rest assured you're in good company. But we still have to talk about it. So join me, take your hands away from your eyes, take that smirk off your face, and let's talk about sex.

Here is a very typical conversation that happens in a couple's first therapy session:

> *Me: How is your sexual relationship?*
>
> *Husband (jumping in to answer, on the edge of his seat for the first time): I mean, of course I wish it happened more often. But I get sick of begging and getting shot down. But if I don't ask, it won't happen. She would never initiate.*
>
> *Wife: Well, he's right, I don't. But I can't go from fighting all day or barely talking for days at a time to being ready to have sex. I don't work that way. I have to feel a connection—an emotional connection.*
>
> *Husband: Maybe if we had sex more, you would feel more of a connection—have you thought of that?*
>
> *Wife (to me): He just doesn't understand that this is not how women work! We have to feel connected first!*
>
> *Husband: I just think you aren't even willing to try. You've decided that it's not going to be good, so you don't even try. That's your problem.*

As I hear this conversation unravel in my office for the umpteenth time, I secretly smile—first, because they are in good company and this is totally fixable; and second, because I know they are both right. They are looking for me to say, "Yes, wife, you are absolutely right about this; you *do* need an emotional connection first, and he *does* need to back off until you have connected on every level in a real, solid, genuine, and meaningful way before he expects sex from you." Or, "Yes, husband, you are absolutely right about this; sex is a crucial part of the connection between a husband and wife, and if she wants this emotional connection that she is claiming she is so desperate for, she needs to start anteing up and have sex with you, for goodness' sake. And while we're at it, she needs to start initiating, and often!"

The truth is, they are both right. Their problem is kind of like the chicken-and-egg argument: does a couple get more connected because they have sex, or do they have sex because they are more connected? I believe the answer is "yes." It's annoying, right?

Couples often come to me because they need to fix their sex lives. They want strategies, techniques, a recent copy of *Seven Ways to Reignite Your Sex Life*. According to them, mostly everything else is fine, and everything would be *perfect* if they could just get their sex life figured out.

Here's another truth: no, everything else isn't fine. I don't yet know what a couple's problem is during this first session, but there is a problem somewhere. And it's not necessarily in the bedroom.

Yes—sexual problems are often a symptom of something deeper. They are most often a sign, a suggestion that something else is off. It's rarely, if ever, all about sex. If you think everything would be great if your husband would just lay off and stop pressuring you for sex—it won't. And if you think everything would be resolved if your wife would just give in and have sex with you every day—that won't work, either.

What I observe is that couples who go through the hard work of figuring out how to talk to each other, learning how to talk about hurts, trying to empathize with each other, supporting each other's lives outside of the marriage, working through all their crazy hang-ups to become a place of comfort for each other, taking responsibility for their parts in their problems, and making changes to become transparent to their partner also end up figuring out their sex lives. They come back and tell me, "And our sex life is so much better, too!" Gosh—and we never even had to talk about sex!

The Struggle Is Real

Even though sexual issues are usually a sign of a deeper problem in a marriage, I still have some helpful opinions directly related to how a married couple views sex. Because let's face it, the struggle is real, with life and kids and jobs demanding attention, and by 9:15 p.m., all you want to do is pass out on the couch.

I'm going to be very stereotypical and assume the husband is the one wanting the sex and the wife is the one refusing. (Of course this is not the case for every marriage, but for ease of illustration, I've elected to use this example.) And I'm going to be direct. So get ready.

Husbands—you cannot emotionally ignore your wife all day or all week and then try to have sex with her. And if she feels ignored, she probably does not want to have sex, and she sure as heck doesn't want to initiate. If she gets to the point that she starts to avoid all physicality—all touches, kisses, or pats on the rear—because she is so afraid that you are going to pounce on her, then there is a problem.

One reason for this problem could be that she has had children vying for her attention all day long—hanging off her hip, her leg, her boob; pulling at her hand; tugging at her shirttail. Do you have any idea, husband, what it's like not to be able to remember the last time you could poop without an audience? Do you?! My daughter once sat on the small trash can in front of our toilet and stared at me while I pooped. Maybe your wife had a similar experience today. And then you want to huff and puff and get all whiny because she doesn't want your hands all over her tonight?

If this is your wife's reality, then duck. Seriously! You may need to learn how to bob and weave to avoid her angry swipe. At this stage, even the *thought* of one more person wanting something physical from her is enough to send her through the roof.

And to you poor husbands experiencing this—I'm sorry. You *do* get the shaft during this phase of life. Please give us grace. Because here's the truth of the matter: at times, many women could do without sex altogether. This isn't because you are not attractive enough, manly enough, or desirable enough to interest us. It's just that our experience of sex isn't the same all the time. It can be way more work for us than it is for you, often with way less reward; and the truth is, we might sometimes get the same enjoyment out of a night spent watching really bad reality TV, when we don't have to touch anyone and our brains can just turn to mush. We just don't have the same drive as you. End of story.

That said, our lower libidos don't give us the right to check out of this area of our marriages altogether. We need to make sure you know you are desirable, even if we sometimes cringe at your touch. We need to make sure we do experience you on a physical, intimate, and sexual level. We need to let you know that we miss intimacy when we don't have it, because we miss *you*, we love you, and we *do* find you desirable, even though we don't want to have sex as much as you do.

Now, wives, you can't keep rejecting him or acting miserable during sex. I know you want a super romantic, touchy-feely, sweet sexual experience like the one you watched on *Grey's Anatomy* last night. But this is reality. Your life is not a TV show or a steamy romance novel. Sex doesn't *need* to feel like fireworks, or like a scene out of a Nicholas Sparks novel. It doesn't need to occur only after you have had a truly mind-blowing heart-to-heart conversation during which you've shared the deepest secrets of your childhood and cried in each other's arms. Sometimes it's just something you do that feels nice and reminds your husband that you like him. There do not have to be roses strewn all over the bed. There do not have to be grapes and fine wine awaiting you at the end. Sometimes it's just good ol' fashioned, been-done-a-thousand-times, married sex. And guess what else? Sometimes it can be good, even great, if you continue to work together to figure out what each of you enjoys, even after years and years.

The one thing that drives me nuts is when couples use passionless sex to justify their looming divorce. "We just don't have that passion anymore." You think? Why do you think that is? Is it the three kids, or the stressful careers, or the looming bills, or the fact that you haven't had the bed to yourselves without your four-year-old coming in for the eighty-seventh night straight? Of course you have lost the passion! Join the club of married men and women everywhere! Just because you feel like you've lost your passion doesn't mean you get to sit back, do nothing about it, and complain. No. This is going to take some work, some attitude-shifting, some digging down deep and seeing what you are truly made of. If you do all that, you may even get the passion back—and it will ebb and flow and have highs and lows, just like everything else in a successful marriage.

I've noticed that women, myself included, get upset if we don't have a daily conversation with our spouses to reinforce our emotional connection with them—but we don't like it if they get upset that they don't have sex regularly. Emotional conversation is women's way to connect, and we pout if we don't get it. Well, sex is men's way to connect. They may pout if they don't get it. Someone has to give. I hope both of you do.

I'll say more: sex should *not* feel like a chore. It shouldn't feel like cleaning the toilets. But for many women, it may be more comparable to going to the gym. You dread it. You would much rather lie in bed a bit longer and sleep or scroll through your social media feed than go to a 6:00 a.m. cardio class—but once you drag your tail out of bed, get to the gym, and feel the sweat dripping down and the adrenaline kicking in, it feels good. You always leave feeling glad you went. You didn't want to, but you did anyway—not because it was a chore, and not because someone was standing beside you pleading or threatening to pout if you didn't, but because you knew you should, because a part of you wanted to, and because you knew that once you got there and the music started playing and your muscles got warmed up and you started to feel the endorphins race through your body, it would have a positive impact on your day.

Be Informed About Porn

Husbands, brace yourselves for this next part. It may be harsh, but bear with me: sex should *not* feel like exploitation for your wife.

With all the technology at our fingertips in this day and age, I think we have to talk about pornography when we talk about sex, in a way that we might not have had to thirty years ago—because porn is everywhere, and because it matters. I'm not taking a stance on whether or not I think porn can be viewed safely in moderation, or even be a mutually agreed upon part of a sexual relationship. I'm just asking you to be informed about porn, and to consider the impact it can have on a relationship. A lot of folks don't do this. They assume that all men consume porn (they don't), and that it's totally harmless (it's not).

Now, you may have considered the risks and decided that the benefits outweigh them—and that's fine for you. But like I said, most folks have *not* considered the risks. They have not considered that viewing pornography can alter a person's neurology, attitude, and view of the human body, and lead them to view sex as a mere act, the way animals do.

The truth is, porn objectifies something that is supposed to be sacred and special and private. Worse, it can make you start to question yourself. After watching porn, men may start to question their stamina and their ability to make a woman feel *that way* and look like *that* during sex. Sorry, but it's never gonna happen, buddy—because your bedroom doesn't have a producer, special lighting, and crazy props. Oh, and your wife isn't getting paid.

You are getting older, and things change. Don't make things harder on yourself by watching a stellar young chap who has been taking steroids since he turned twenty.

Many couples come into my office and complain of the husband's inability to "perform" in the bedroom. That apparent inability can feel like a total slap in the face when she later finds him enjoying pornography. It's confusing and insulting. She cannot understand why porn can manage to interest him while she cannot. Most often, these same couples do not know that his inability to perform is often a direct result of his pornography viewing habits. They have desensitized him to common depictions of intercourse and created a need in his brain for more risqué, more graphic images to achieve the same level of excitement. It's almost like drinking. If you drink often, you have to start drinking more and more to get the same buzz. The feeling you used to get after drinking a few beers now comes only after you drink a few more beers, some wine, and a nice stiff cocktail.

I hope you are still bearing with me, husbands, because I know this sounds harsh. I promise I'm not singling you out—I really let the women have it when I discussed criticism in Chapter Three. Keep reading; you're doing great.

Your sweet wives are likely already critiquing every part of their aging bodies. They can't compete with the near-perfect models found in pornographic videos and magazines—and neither, in point of fact, can you. After all, can you truly convince me that you don't feel subpar when you compare those airbrushed bodies to your own physique?

I sure know how I feel about my aging post-baby body. I know that even though my daughter is cute as can be, I almost cried when she asked me, "Mom, why does your belly button look like that? I mean, it's all stretched out." (Yes, I did leap out of my skin and scream, *"Because of you and your sister! That's why!"* Not my best parenting moment.) I also know the way I feel when

I see Kate Upton gracing the cover of *US Weekly* as I check out at the grocery store. Can you truly convince me that these videos, images, and scenes that become etched in your brain (they do) don't make you question yourself or your wife?

My final point (I'm almost done, husbands, I promise!) is for those of you who look over at your spouse and think, *I'm just not attracted to her anymore.* That's *fine.* That can happen. Attraction can absolutely change. You may have noticed how the skin under your wife's arm, once supple and firm, now sways like a flag in the breeze. But did you also notice how sweetly she looked at your son when he skinned his knees? When she tenderly wiped his tears and told him everything was going to be okay—did you notice that, too?

The cold truth is, pornography can really start to change your focus, and cause you to objectify and sexualize your wife—and not in a good way.

Okay, you made it through my rant. I'll take a few deep breaths and move on.

Women and Desire—It's Tricky

Women, it's your turn. For many of you, your husband wants you; he desires you. This is great news! He wants to have sex with you! If this is your reality, congratulations! It's not everyone's. Think about how you would feel if he did not want you, didn't desire you, didn't want to jump all over you after seeing you in that low-cut top.

It's time to embrace his desire for you. You can't complain that he never notices your new shirt and then, in the next breath, complain, "Just because I put on this new shirt, it doesn't give you the right to pounce!" You *want* your husband to want you—and even though ten years may have passed since you got together with your spouse—or twenty, or even thirty—I don't think the desire to impress has to go out the window.

I remember how much I would hem and haw about what to wear when I went on my first dates with my husband. I still care if my husband thinks I'm desirable—contrary to what my tousled hair and snot-covered Old Navy T-shirt might communicate to him when he comes home. That means I often choose to make the effort to be flirty and romantic—not because he expects it, but because I *want* to.

For example, my husband *hates* it when I wear gray clothes. Unfortunately, gray workout and sleep attire seems to be my specialty. So guess what? I save my favorite cozy, raggedy old gray shorts for nights he is out of town. Then I sleep in them in all their glory, and smile as I drift off. But I choose not to wear them in front of him—again, not because I have to, but because I think it's important to continue to make an effort.

Recently, I went away for a girls' weekend in the mountains with my dear friends of over twenty years. We came back to our nice little cabin in the woods after a day spent wine-tasting. My super cute and trendy friend changed out of her fashionable chambray dress and threw on her pajamas. A little hottie patottie mamma instantly became an eighty-year-old grandma. Think *The Golden Girls*—and not hot and flirty Blanche, but cranky Sophia.

Now, I love that my friends are so comfortable with each other that we don't dress to impress, but we wanted to make sure that this same spirit didn't carry into her marriage.

Us: Ummmm . . . no. Not okay.

Friend: What? It's comfortable.

Us: For sure, but we hope you don't ever, ever show this to your husband. And if you already have, burn it immediately!

You may not want to jump his bones; it may be too early for you to appreciate his touch again after a pregnancy; you may have lost steam after twenty years. But you need to do *something*—something to let him know that you desire him, that he is still attractive in your eyes, that you do think of him sexually (or at least that you *want* to), that you care about this part of your relationship, and that you can't and don't want to live without it, even if your drive has gone to crap.

Lastly, if your level of sexual desire has changed through the years, relax. You are totally normal! So many factors can affect sexual desire: breastfeeding, painful sex after childbirth, hormone changes, trauma, a decrease in emotional connection with your partner, work stress, grief, anxiety. Exhaustion and the fear of waking a child can also come into play—and these certainly don't set a great mood for desire. There is also a chance that sex has become less pleasurable for you over time, and therefore, you want it less.

If your desire has changed, I urge you and your spouse to educate yourselves on sexuality. Like many other aspects of our physical health, sex can be surprisingly unintuitive. For example, you may know you need to eat healthily, but you had to learn exactly what good nutrition is. You know that you should get plenty of sleep at night, but if sleeping has been a struggle for you, you may have had to learn calming techniques to enable yourself to sleep through the night. Similarly, you know *how* to have sex—but you may need to learn more about how your and your partner's bodies respond to sexual stimuli in order to improve your sex life. If you're like a lot of people, the only places you or your partner have learned about sex may have been through your middle-school health classes, casual conversations, and entertainment-focused media. These are not reliable sources!

Sex educator Emily Nagoski explains that we all have sexual accelerators—things that turn us on and motivate us to have and enjoy sex—and sexual brakes, things that decrease our desire for sex.[3] Learn about yours. Learn about your partner's. Learn how your accelerators and brakes have changed over the years, after childbirth, a medical diagnosis, or a trauma. What feels good now? What doesn't? If desire is an issue for you as a couple, grab a copy of Emily's book and read it together.

But We *Have* Talked About It!

If you feel sex is an issue in your relationship, you need to talk about it—no two ways about it. In this moment, though, you may be reacting to that suggestion the same way many of my couples have responded:

Couple 1:

> *Me: It sounds like you need to talk about this problem together.*

> *Wife (to me): We have talked about it! It hasn't changed a thing!*

---

3. Nagoski, Emily. *Come as You Are: The Surprising New Science That Will Transform Your Sex Life.* New York: Simon & Schuster, 2015.

Me: Oh, really? Tell me about these conversations.

Wife: Well, we talked about how he needs to get checked out, because obviously something is wrong. Finally he did, and they found out he has low testosterone, so he took care of that. But things still seem to be an issue, so we talked about what else we need to do to fix things. He just doesn't seem interested in any solutions.

Couple 2:

Me: It sounds like you need to talk about this problem together.

Wife (to me): I'm so sick of talking about it! I feel like it's all I hear about!

Me: Oh, really? Tell me about these conversations.

Wife: He knows exactly how I feel about it. We have talked over and over about how he always asks to be intimate super late at night, when I'm so tired from my day and the kids that all I want is to go to sleep. And then he gets all mad and pouty, and I tell him that it doesn't make me want to have sex with him when he pouts all the time.

Husband: Oh, come on. When is the last time I got mad about it? I stopped caring whether you reject me or not a long time ago.

To the wife whose husband's desire has decreased or performance has changed: I understand how confusing it can be for a woman to see these changes in her husband. It can even feel like rejection. You may hear your friends complaining about their husbands' overactive sex drives and wonder, sometimes out loud to your husband, "What's wrong with you?!"

But I can tell you this: nothing will shut down this conversation, make this topic completely off-limits, and continue to create confusion and distance more than the question, "Do you need to get checked out? Obviously something is wrong with you!" It would not be helpful to say, "Let's figure out how to fix you," or "Let's figure out what unresolved deep-seated issues you have that may be making you impotent."

Instead, I recommend a softer, gentler, and safer approach. Before you broach the subject, put on some super-gentle, plushy kid gloves. I know this can be hard to do, especially when you are feeling rejected. Nevertheless, try: "I'm starting to feel a bit confused, and have started to wonder if you don't desire me anymore. I know I'm not a man, so I can't truly understand, but I know that things can change, and it is often hard to talk about that. But I'm all ears. I'm interested in figuring out some things together. I want you to feel safe talking with me about this. I really think it could help."

You may be tempted to send your husband to an array of doctors for immediate testosterone testing, in the hope of getting quick results. I'm not suggesting avoiding medical intervention—I'm just saying, first and foremost, try to become a safe place to explore what's changed for him, with him. Many factors can affect a man's confidence and desire, from aging to medical conditions to stress.

One more thing, ladies. Go back and read Chapter Three, the one about criticism. If your husband is one among the ranks of men who feel like nothing they can do is good enough for their partners, it is quite common for this attitude to spill over into the bedroom. It is just one more place he is letting you down, getting it wrong, failing you. The fear and anxiety that come with trying to avoid criticism do not allow for a super-sexy, romantic experience. In fact, that type of anxiety can lead to a lot of performance issues.

If you want to find out whether this point applies to your marriage, you may ask him, "Do you ever feel anxious when it comes to sex? Do I ever make you feel worried, concerned, not good enough in our sexual relationship?" If he gives any indication that this is the case, please respond with, "Thank you so much for telling me. What do you need me to do to help you in those moments?"

If, on the other hand, you are a woman who wants a more connected experience with your husband, you can start by telling him, "I'm starting to feel distant from you during sex. It's almost like you don't even see me when we have sex. It's really important that I feel you want to be with me during those moments. I know you love me, but it's important that I feel connected in those moments. I think it would help if you . . . " Then give some suggestions. He's not a mind reader; he doesn't know what you mean when you say you want to feel "connected." He needs some guidance. Do you need him to make eye contact? Do you need to cuddle before or after; do you need to kiss often and throughout; do you need to take it slow? Do you need to talk about your days first, to help yourselves feel more emotionally connected before initiating sex? Or do you need to feel relaxed at the end of the night, and to have some time specifically set aside for intimacy? If you do need to set some time aside, you may need to take the initiative to do this. Don't rely on him, because he may try once—and if you refuse him at the time he suggests, he probably won't try again.

If you are a man who feels rejected, I want you to talk to your wife about how that feels for you, too. Before you do, however, consider this one caveat: if the *only* need you ever bring up in your marriage is your desire for more sex, you may not find her very receptive. In other words, if your wife feels that you do not care about her emotional desires in this marriage, and if she feels that you are only happy and content as long as you get sex, she may not be open or willing to work on this problem with you.

In cases like this, it may help to let her know that you are eager to fulfill her emotional desires, too. It may help if you also turn to her to meet your emotional needs, not just your physical ones. Yes, this may mean talking about your feelings and sharing how you feel. But once you have done that, it will be a lot safer to say, "I know it's important to make sure our emotional needs are met, but is it okay if we also talk about some physical desires?" Then you can explain, "I'm starting to feel rejected, and have started to wonder if you don't want me anymore. I know you are tired; I know the kids are hanging on you all day, and I'm trying really hard not to take it personally—but sometimes I do. I start to worry that you don't want me, don't desire me. And that actually makes me sad." Ask, "What do you need from me to help you feel more motivated to have sex with me? Is there anything I can do to help you enjoy it more? It would mean a lot to me if you would initiate sex at times, and it hurts me to feel like you aren't enjoying it—like you are just doing it because you feel you have to. It's important to me that you are enjoying, too. I'm all ears. What do you think would help?"

I hope that with this change in tone relieving her of any blame, she will share some ideas with you. If she does—by all means, try them! And if those particular ideas don't help, talk some more, and try some more things. Your sex life isn't a one-stop shop. It's complex. It might actually take some work. Stop neglecting this part of your marriage.

In Chapter Nine, we explored strategies for getting to the root of the problems in your marriage. I have seen amazing success for couples who have applied these strategies to their sexual relationships.

One couple I worked with, Ben and Amanda, explained that they were struggling with Ben's lack of sexual desire. Here is how their quarterly fight went down during one of our first sessions:

Me: How was your weekend getaway?

Ben: I thought we had a good time, for the most part.

Amanda: I guess so.

Me: Tell me about it.

Amanda: I mean, it was fine. We had a nice dinner and went on a boat ride. It was all fine. Until we got back to the room and he went to sleep, as usual. But he's probably going to be mad I'm even bringing it up now. He hates to talk about it. I'm just supposed to be content with our nonexistent sex life.

Ben: I'm trying to get things sorted out. I went to the doctor like you asked me to and got tested. I've started taking the medication he prescribed. What more do you want?

Amanda: Right. After years of me complaining, he finally made an appointment. I guess he's taking the

*medication. I don't know—he doesn't ever want to talk
about it. It's obviously not that important to him. I mean,
it's taken this long for him to do anything about it.*

I got to know this couple a bit more in subsequent sessions, and got to understand their relationship outside the bedroom. And wouldn't you know it—the dynamics were exactly the same. The same types of interactions that plagued them in their daily life also crept into their sexual relationship.

Because I had the privilege of becoming quite the expert on their negative patterns outside the bedroom, I could more easily help them understand how things went amiss in the bedroom. As we peeled back the layers of this seemingly straightforward problem—*she wants to have sex, and he doesn't, because he has "issues"*—we found the *real* problem:

Me: How was the week?

Ben: I might as well go ahead and tell you, because I know she is going to bring it up. It was her birthday this week. I sent the kids to Grandma's house so we could have the house to ourselves for the night. Long story short, we tried to be intimate, it wasn't working, she got mad, and then I got mad and left the room. We spent the night apart.

Amanda: Exactly. He left, because it's all about him. He doesn't care about me and what I need.

Me (to Ben): What happened after you left the room?

Ben: I don't know. I guess I felt embarrassed. It's humiliating, you know? I had done the things I thought I needed to do. I went to the doctor, I took the medication he prescribed, I tried to create a romantic situation. I just wanted it to be perfect. When it didn't go how I wanted it to, I was so disappointed and upset. I don't know how much longer she'll be willing to put up with this.

Me (to Ben): You wonder if she will leave you?

Ben: Sometimes. I just know I need to give this to her, and I feel like I can't. It's the worst feeling in the world. I just wish it could be easy for me, like it used to be. I wish I could satisfy her like I used to.

Me (to Amanda): How do you feel as you hear this?

Amanda: It makes me sad. I don't want him to feel he is letting me down. I don't want him to feel embarrassed.

Me (to Amanda): You said it seemed like he doesn't care about you in those moments. How does it seem now?

Amanda: I see that he cares. I actually hate that he puts that much pressure on himself. I would be content with just a good cuddle and a movie. I just want to be together and connected. That's what's most important.

Ben (to Amanda): I do put a lot of pressure on myself to get things right for you. I build up the moment in my mind until it feels so big, it makes me anxious. I start to get scared that things may not go well.

Me (to Ben): What happens when you get scared like that?

Ben: When we start to get intimate, I feel so anxious about things not going well that it can become all I think about. And when I'm feeling so anxious, I can't concentrate on her.

Me: It's the anxiety of disappointing her or losing her that creeps into those moments?

Ben: Absolutely.

Amanda (to Ben): Babe, I'm not going anywhere! I just complain about it because I do want a sexual connection with you. And it seems sometimes that you don't care about our sex life, and that you don't care about my needs.

Me (to Amanda): That's what you tell yourself—that he doesn't care about you and your needs?

Amanda: Well, yes. That, and sometimes . . . I start to wonder whether he has a hard time being sexual with me because he no longer desires me. I start to wonder whether he has lost his attraction to me.

Me (to Amanda): Have you been able to share this with him before? This fear you have that he no longer desires you?

Amanda: No, I'm afraid of what I'll hear. Or that he will just get mad.

Me (to Ben): Do you get angry right now when you hear that?

Ben: No, just the opposite. I hate that my "issues" have made her feel that way. It couldn't be further from the truth. (to Amanda): I do desire you! Actually, it's because I desire you so much and I care so much about pleasing you that I get myself all worked up. I get so anxious about doing things so perfectly for you. If I could change things, I would. I just don't know what to do.

Me (to Ben): What happens when you hear her say that she isn't going anywhere, that she just wants to be with you?

Ben: It feels good. I can feel my anxiety go down immediately.

Me: Do you think you could ask for her reassurance when you start to feel anxious?

Ben: I've never thought to do that, but yes, I think I could.

Me (to Amanda): Would you be open to talking about ways to reassure him, comfort him, connect with him, that may help in those moments?

Amanda: Absolutely.

Me (to Ben): Would you be open to continuing to reassure her of your desire for her, and of your desire to please her?

Ben: Of course.

Now Ben and Amanda are ready to tackle their "sexual" issues, because their emotional connection has been restored. They have allowed themselves to be vulnerable and share their fears and hurts regarding their sexual relationship. Each has done so in a way that allowed their partner to listen and truly hear them. Each has done so in a way that made their partner feel cared for and loved. Now their partner is no longer the enemy. Sex is no longer a threat to the relationship. With the security of the relationship intact, they can brainstorm freely. Without the fear that a failed sexual experience will cause their relationship to self-destruct, they can more easily engage in finding creative solutions through trial and error. At times, they can even find humor and laugh together about "failed" attempts. They can use this "issue" as a way to become more emotionally intimate with each other. And then a magical thing will happen: once they become more emotionally intimate, the sexual intimacy will soon follow.

Most Couples Come to Therapy Too Late

There is one final truth I feel I must reveal. I hate this one. It pains me more than all the other truths I've shared in this book. It makes me want to sink into my therapist's chair and drop my head in defeat. When I encounter a couple struggling with this truth, it makes me wish I had magic wands, lotions, and potions that could turn everything around.

But I don't—and so this is the reality, the terrible truth: most couples come to therapy too late.

When I encounter a couple who has waited too long to come to therapy, I find myself sadly wondering, *Why now? Now, when you have wounded each other so badly; now, when you have lost respect for each other; now, when this has been going on for so long—why are you just now coming in?*

Unfortunately, the reason they are coming in is usually because one person has finally thrown in the towel. They have given up, emotionally and sometimes even physically, and their desperate partner has been left scrambling and begging, "Please, at least try therapy!" So they come.

And I can see the sad truth, which is that the partner is only coming to say they tried. "See, we even tried marriage counseling, and even that didn't work! What else do you want me to do?" The partner has already checked out, and often there is nothing I can do about that. Believe me, if I could change that by standing on my head while singing "The Star-Spangled Banner," I would. But your best chance for change comes when you start early enough, while you still have respect and love for each other somewhere deep down inside. Don't wait until it's too late.

What About Counseling?

How do you know if it's time for counseling? There is no definite answer—but I do know that your marriage does not have to be in turmoil or crisis for counseling to be of help. If you are feeling disconnected, unloved, uncared for, or emotionally unsafe; if you feel little confidence in your ability to talk about difficult things as a couple and find some resolution; if you are starting to feel hopeless, lonely, depressed, anxious, or helpless when it comes to your marriage—if any one of these things is happening, counseling can help.

If I called my husband to ask him whether I should take our daughter to the doctor when I suspected she was developing an ear infection for the hundredth time, he would give me the same response he gave me the first ninety-nine times: "It can't hurt. You might as well find out if there is anything more to it." The same thinking applies here: it can't hurt. Just as almost everyone occasionally falls under the weather, no marriage is perfect. If you start feeling nervous about some aspect of your marriage, it's almost always worth coming in for a "checkup" to find out whether that aspect is worth worrying about, or whether your dynamics might just require a little tweaking.

When seeking help, it's important to know that not all

therapists can help you in the ways you need. I'm not trying to discredit any therapist out there—there are a lot of different types of issues and clients *I'm* not the most qualified to work with. Instead, I refer these clients to therapists who *are* more qualified. You have to find someone who specializes in the problems you're having. I see a lot of clients who have tried going to all sorts of therapists to work through their marital woes. But that is like going to a general practitioner instead of an oncologist to treat cancer—and while general practitioners may be amazingly knowledgeable and helpful about lots of different things, they aren't cancer specialists. Similarly, not every therapist has been specifically trained to deal with marital strife. It's a specialty.

To find a specialist, ask around. Talk to your primary care physician, your OB-GYN, your dentist, your dermatologist—heck, you could even ask your florist. Better yet, talk to your friends. You will be amazed at how many of them have seen a marriage counselor at some point, or know someone who has.

As I have mentioned, I am a *huge* supporter of Dr. Sue Johnson's emotionally focused couples therapy (EFT). You can find a nearby therapist who is trained in EFT at www.ICEEFT.com. Check out some bios and profiles of therapists in your area. Call them. Determine their availability. Make an appointment. And if you don't have a positive experience—if you don't walk away feeling like the therapist "gets" you or your relationship, or if you don't feel you are being understood and listened to—find someone else. Sometimes you have to shop around to find a good fit. That's okay. You probably didn't jump in and buy the first car you test-drove, either. This might take a little effort, too. But it's worth it.

And it's worth commitment, too. Whatever you do, don't go

to couples therapy a mere three times and say, "It's not working; nothing is changing; we must be irretrievably broken." That's like going to the gym and saying after three sessions, "It's not working! I haven't lost the weight and I still don't see a six-pack." It's like saying, "He went to five golf lessons, and he still can't sink the putt! He still hits it into the woods like he always has, and sometimes he even misses the ball altogether!" Of course he does! Golf is hard—frustratingly so. I started taking lessons years ago, and on most days, I still can't play worth a darn. But at least I'm out there, swinging and missing and then trying again.

It's not uncommon for a couple who has been struggling for fifteen years to come back after five sessions and say, "It's not working; he's not even doing anything different!" Whoa, Nelly! He has been doing things a certain way for fifteen years in this marriage, with probably another fifteen years of the same madness before he married you. Making positive changes takes work, my friends—but it's your marriage, for goodness' sake!

I'll never stop being amazed at how much money a couple will be willing to spend in a contentious divorce, while they balk at the idea of spending even a fraction of that on marriage counseling to give themselves a chance. If your marriage is on the rocks or in shambles, it's going to take some work and sacrifice to fix it. So if you really want to save your relationship, don't take that big trip this year. Take a break from fancy dinners, and use that money to do something different. Use it to find someone who can help.

How to Handle Your Kids

If you believe your marriage is in danger of failing, you need to make fixing it a top priority. You need to make it more important than playing in your weekly tennis match, or getting your kids to their soccer game. After all, watching their mother and father handle the pain and heartache of a divorce would be far more devastating for your kids than missing a game, or five— or even all of them.

There is no harm (actually, quite the opposite is true) in going to your kids and saying, "I'm sure you have seen Mommy and Daddy fighting. Well, we are going to talk to someone who can help us. Because we love each other so much, we are going to let someone help us be a better husband and wife. And I hope that if you are fighting with your husband or wife one day, you will let someone help you, too! It's so important!

"So, because of this, we are going to let you ride to and from your Friday soccer games with your friends, and we are going to have to miss those games. Just for a little while, until we learn how to make our home a happier place. We love you so much, and we are willing to do anything to make sure our home is happy. I can't wait to hear all about your game! Go get 'em!"

If you really want to save your marriage, you need to make sacrifices until things have turned around. Then you can take the big trip, go to the fancy dinners, and cheer on your kids at their soccer games. And it will be a lot more fun, I promise.

The best thing you can do for your kids—more important than signing them up for soccer or dance class, more important than reading bedtime stories or helping them with their homework, more important than making sure they have perfect matching outfits to wear for those family portraits that will adorn the front of this year's Christmas cards, which you are secretly hoping your friends and family will look at with envy, thinking, *Now, that is a cute family!*—more important than all these actions is showing your kids what a healthy marriage looks like.

Notice I didn't say, "Showing your kids what a *happy* marriage looks like." I didn't say your kids need to see marriage as something that's all smiles and sunshine. I said, "Showing your kids what a *healthy* marriage looks like." A healthy marriage can include conflict. Mistakes. Mishaps. Misunderstandings. Miscommunication. But it should also include a mutual mission to try harder, to learn new things, work through conflict, and talk things out.

Your marriage should be the center of your family. And if you are religious, then God should be the center of your marriage. Do you know what this means? If God is the center and your marriage is next, this means your kids are in third place! Third! Don't operate as if they are first.

If your instinct is to say, "I may be a crappy husband, but I'm a great dad"—impossible! You may do some amazing things for your kids; I'm not doubting that. But the most amazing act of fatherhood is to respect your children's mother. Love her. Do it openly, even when it's hard. Even when she acts unlovable because she is so exhausted from all she does for your family.

Wives—you may joke and say, "My husband and I haven't talked in weeks, months, or years. But who has time for that? I've got three kids to raise, swim lessons to get to, dentist appointments to make, and school supplies to purchase. And tomorrow is school picture day, and I need to go online and pay seventy dollars for overnight shipping to get that perfect Hanna Andersson dress, so that everyone can look at my daughter and say, 'Mom, you did so good, she looked so adorable!'"

Guess what? She looks adorable because she is. She could wear a grocery bag and look adorable, because she is that darn cute. Now grab your best hand-me-down out of the closet, set it out for tomorrow, and go snuggle with your husband! Let him know he is more important than buying perfect clothes that your son will ruin within minutes when he jumps in the first mud puddle he sees.

How to Handle Your Spouse

Now, you can't go to counseling to change your spouse, either. Couples therapy is not meant to change only one person. It's meant to change both of you—to change "us." Because guess what? No therapist can make him stop watching football incessantly, start cleaning up after himself, or extend his arm an extra two feet to put his dirty dish in the dishwasher and not the sink. I certainly can't. And if I could, there would be no way you could get an appointment with me. I would be charging $500,000 per hour and have a miles-long line of couples outside my office, waiting to get in.

I can't change him. I can't change her. But I *can* help you change your conversations, and so can a lot of other marriage counselors. And if we can change those, *everything* can change.

Now, how can you get your spouse to join you without kicking and screaming? You can start by making sure you aren't going to counseling so that the counselor can tell your partner how wrong he or she is and how right you are. You have to own your piece of the struggle. You have to acknowledge that this is a two-way street, and that you have your part in the problem, too. You have to tell your spouse that you love them, that you are in pain, and that because the relationship is so important to you, you want help working through this pain and this struggle in the most healthy, helpful, and loving way possible—because you don't want to get this wrong. This marriage is too important for you to take a gamble, because you love your partner and don't want to hurt them anymore, and you don't want them to hurt you anymore, either. If you make an appointment, will they come with you? Tell them straight out: "It would mean the world to me if you would come. Please? For us?"

A friend once came to me because she had been hurt very deeply by her husband of fifteen years, the father of her three kids. Her trust was shattered. They were trying counseling and reconciliation. He kept getting upset with her because she was not prioritizing the relationship. She would go out with her friends and come home late, missing dates they had scheduled.

She called me to vent: "How dare he complain? He's the one who hurt me! He's the one who destroyed our marriage. I'm sick of hearing how he doesn't feel like a priority. Obviously I wasn't a priority when he did what he did! I think I deserve to be able to go out and have fun with my friends!"

I think most friends would have told her, "You're right!" (She was.) "He did this to you, and if you want to hang out with your friends, that is your right! He should just be thankful that you haven't already left his butt on the curb." I could have said those things, too. They were true. He had hurt her severely, in such a way that trust might never be restored.

But there was another truth. I knew that a part of my friend, who was hurting so deeply and had threatened divorce a million times in the last four months—just a small part—wanted to stay married. So I said, "Dear, sweet friend, this marriage is not going to fix itself. I know you would rather have fun with your friends than deal with this big pile of BS on your doorstep. But your marriage will not survive if you keep ignoring the work that needs to be done. If there is even a teeny, tiny part of you that wants to fix this, that wants to stay married, you have to sacrifice. And it's not fair! He was the one who hurt you, and you are the one sacrificing. But it's time to put on your big-girl pants and start prioritizing this relationship. Furthermore, you should take responsibility and apologize for not doing so when you missed your date with him last night."

Several months after we had this conversation, I received a voicemail from this friend. She was coming home from her six-teen-year anniversary dinner. Her message was filled with grati-tude and joy. She thanked me for giving her permission to fight for a marriage that had caused her so much pain. She told me that thanks to their sacrifices, counseling, date nights, conver-sations, and tears, their marriage was the best it had ever been. She couldn't believe it. She was scared she was going to wake up tomorrow and find that this had all been a dream. Things were that good.

Should I Stay or Go?

How do you know if you should stay or go?

This is a hard question—one that causes most spouses to break out in a cold sweat or panic attack. This question can be all-con-suming and suck all the joy out of life. But I'll share a few pointers. First, no one else can make this decision for you. No one else knows exactly how it feels to be you. No one else knows the full history of your relationship, the highest of its highs and the lowest of its lows. No one else knows the full extent of the heart-break or the tender moments. Only *you* do. That's why this deci-sion is ultimately between your gut, your heart, your head, and your Higher Power.

But that does *not* mean that you should make this decision alone. On the contrary! Seek guidance. Seek counsel. But be careful in this. Be careful whom you choose to confide in, whom you allow to influence you, whom you choose to listen to. Don't seek out your best buddy, who is still bitter and angry over the fact that his wife left him for another man. Don't seek out the coworker who has been married three times and is pissed off that her newest husband is just as worthless and selfish as the others. Don't consult your best friend if that friend is having an emotional affair with her neighbor. Be selective. Find someone you trust—someone who has a marriage you respect or a position that you trust, such as a pastor, mentor, or counselor. Find someone who can see both sides.

Sometimes you have to fight for your marriage. Sometimes, you may feel like you are the only one bearing the burdens or making the sacrifices. But even if the effort you put into fixing your relationship is entirely one-sided, you should feel good that you are trying so hard to fight for your marriage. You deserve to feel good about your hard work. You never know—you may just turn your whole relationship around.

It can happen. I watch these little miracles happen all the time. And let me tell you, it never gets old.

Marriages never stop being saved. I'm hoping yours can be one of them.

Acknowledgments

On the day of our tenth wedding anniversary, I told my husband I wanted to write a book about marriage. (I was 85 percent sure I meant it.) I had no idea how much help I would need to accomplish this feat. Publishing this book would have never been possible without the people who helped me, and I want to say thank you.

First and foremost, I want to thank my perfectly chaotic family: my husband, Chad; and my amazing daughters, Brooklyn and Reagan. Chad, you are my fierce and constant supporter. Not only have you corralled the kids when I needed to work and listened to my endless struggles with title changes and chapter headings, but you allowed me to put our marriage on paper for the world to see. Thank you for being a husband and father I am proud to describe in these pages.

I feel so much gratitude toward the clients who have sat in my office and allowed me into their private lives. Every single one of you has touched my life in a profound way. You have taught me more about love and human nature than a textbook ever could. I hope the invaluable lessons each of you has taught me about marriage are represented well in this book.

As a marriage counselor, I've experienced the luxury of being trained by and working alongside some of the most talented therapists in my field: Dr. Marcus Earle, Dr. Everett Bailey, Dr. Morgan Francis, Shanna Larson-Paola, Doug Withrow, Mark Bell, and the rest of the staff at Psychological Counseling Services in Scottsdale, Arizona. I became the therapist I am today because of the influence of each one of you.

I am grateful to the entire EFT community of amazing couples therapists, many of whom have trained me and helped me hone my craft of saving marriages. I was introduced to Dr. Sue Johnson's emotionally focused couples therapy (EFT) early in my career, and it quickly became the foundation of my therapy. Dr. David Weinstock, Dr. Vickie Spitzer, and Dr. Scott Baker have influenced both my writing and therapy in immeasurable ways. Thank you for the hours of consultation, guidance, support, laughter, and tears.

Being friends with a marriage counselor/author is as courageous as being married to one. Courtney Owens, Trisha Smith, Carrie Johnstone, Angie Fletcher, Cassidy MacKay, Jillian Angel, Daphne Robertson, April Poling, Amy Piland, Kitty Ivey, and Kellie Delapp have been my closest friends since our days at UNC-Chapel Hill. Thank you for remaining my friends even though I write about you! In particular, a few of these people have made specific contributions to this book. Courtney, thank you for the hours you spent on the phone encouraging me and helping me brainstorm. Trisha, thank you for our brainstorming lunches and your top-notch public relations knowledge. And to Carrie: you have been so supportive of me with your feedback, your hospitality, and your confidence in me. Thank you.

As I dove into writing this book, many friends shared their own gifts for writing with me. Katherine Bartis: how lucky I am to have a friend with your grammatical expertise. You are conscientious, diligent, and brilliant. I can say with absolute certainty that I would have never finished this book without you. Thank you for being as invested in, excited about, and devoted to this book as I have been. Tommy Johnstone: thank you for being the first person to read and fine-tune my original manuscript. Betsy Thorpe: with your expert editorial help early on, you gave me the direction and confidence I needed when my book was in its infant stage. Lastly, Joy Callaway: being the neighbor of a talented author such as yourself clearly has its perks! Thank you for your wisdom in navigating the world of publishing.

Thank you to my family—my parents Robert and Cathy, and my brother Kenny and sister-in-law Heather. You each have provided an amazing example of how to be a committed, loving, and devoted spouse. I am so grateful to have family who support me like you do, and who have taught me the value of marriage.

Finally, thank you to the team at Brandylane and Belle Isle Books—Robert H. Pruett, Erin Harpst, and Annie Tobey. Through your collaborative spirit, you have made the experience of editing and publishing this book an absolute joy.

About the Author

Lori Epting is a licensed clinical mental health counselor in North Carolina. She holds a master's in counseling, and has focused her professional training on couples and addiction therapy. She is certified in the Advanced Training in Problematic Sexual Behaviors (ATPSB) program, and formally trained in the professionally accepted and empirically validated treatment model of emotionally focused couples therapy (EFT).

Lori currently works in private practice, treating couples and families at Lori Epting Counseling, PLLC, where she specializes in marital therapy using EFT. You can read more about Lori and how she helps couples navigate the chaos of modern marriage at her professional blog, "Marriage Sense: Making Sense of Modern Marriage" (MarriageSense.org). She is a topic expert for GoodTherapy.org, contributing articles about marriage and addiction.

Lori lives in Charlotte, NC, with her husband and their two daughters.

CPSIA information can be obtained
at www.ICGtesting.com
Printed in the USA
FSHW010523081020
74609FS